AF322574

Praise for Corporate Campfire Stories

"As someone who's been in leadership for decades, I can say that the lessons in this book are spot-on. It offers a unique perspective on leadership—grounded in experience but with a forward-thinking approach that makes it relevant to aspiring leaders of today. And while the lessons of the past continue to be relevant, what I especially appreciate is the focus on the future. It doesn't just tell you how to be a good leader today, but how to prepare for tomorrow's challenges. It's a refreshing approach to leadership that blends practical advice with long-term vision."

—Tom McInerney
CEO, Genworth

"I know Brian as an approachable and relatable leader who connects with you as a person, not just a professional. He takes genuine interest in understanding you—listening more than he speaks, ensuring that you're heard, understood, and matter. Reading the stories in this book feels like talking with a sage and insightful family member who only wants the best for you. Candid, yet gentle. Thorough, yet clear."

—Ron Edwards
Senior Director for Talent, Fortune 100 Financial Services Company

"As a woman in tech, I found Brian's book both practical and deeply inspiring. It feels like having a trusted mentor by your side—offering honest insight, real-world wisdom, and thoughtful guidance on navigating growth and leadership with purpose. I especially appreciate how he balances the technical side with people management, showing how to lead with empathy while staying grounded in results. It's a rare combination of heart and practicality that truly resonates."

—Amy T. (34)
Digital Platform Manager, Fortune 10 Company

"*Corporate Campfire Stories* nails what most leadership books miss: the messy, human middle where people, process and results meet. The stories are practical, punchy and immediately useful; perfect for emerging leaders who want to turn real world friction into forward motion."

—Ahmad O. (38)
AI and Machine Learning Leader, International Consulting Firm

"As a finance professor, I know that my MBA and Executive MBA students crave practical wisdom, not just theory. Brian Haendiges delivers. His story-based lessons are consistently a massive hit when shared with my classes. It's fantastic to have those real-world stories captured in this book, providing accessible examples in practical leadership in an invaluable guide for emerging leaders."

—Pete Vatev
Assistant Professor of Finance,
Virginia Commonwealth University School of Business

"This book is a master class in real-world leadership, filled with engaging stories, hard-won lessons, and practical insights every emerging leader can apply. A must-read for anyone looking to grow their impact and navigate their career with confidence."

—Jeff L. (31)
Senior Associate, Investment Technology Firm

"This is more than just another business book. The guidance for advancing your career is rooted in engaging and memorable stories, each giving a framework for how a fundamental principle can be applied, with practical next steps. The powerful imagery of Brian's stories sticks with you, and I've both used and repeated his advice to countless aspiring actuaries over the years."

—Amanda Hug
Past President, Society of Actuaries

"*Corporate Campfire Stories* is a must-read for anyone looking to enhance their leadership skills, and every aspiring leader in today's corporate environment should read it. The practical advice is rooted in real-world experiences, and I've seen the techniques in the book work. Whether you're looking to strengthen your communication, influence, or team dynamics, these actionable insights will immediately improve your leadership abilities."

—Elaine Sarsynski
Board Member, Multiple Organizations

"*Corporate Campfire Stories* brilliantly demonstrates the power of storytelling to illustrate the realities of navigating one's career. As someone at the midpoint of their corporate journey, and focused on advancement, I found the lessons incredibly relevant and thought-provoking. Each story is not only insightful but also engaging, making it a truly enjoyable read that leaves you with actionable advice."

—Matt G. (33)
Brand Manager, Global Consumer Products Company

"The distinction between managers and leaders is critical, and this book will create better leaders. A manager dictates and expects people to follow. A leader sets the vision, establishes buy-in and a trusted relationship, and convinces people to follow them in spite of uncertainty. Brian's book is a practical, easy reading guide to how so many opportunities in your life and work, and how you relate to them, can make you a leader."

—Barbara March
CEO and Owner, My Corporate Ally

"Brian Haendiges is an ENGAGING storyteller in *Corporate Campfire Stories*! He weaves captivating, relevant stories that bring leadership lessons vividly to life while prompting heartfelt self-reflection to align what truly matters with how and where we show up each day. His guidance inspires us to pause, act with a deep compassion for others, and create the space to become our best selves."

—Darrin Tulley
Chief Possibilities Officer, Ignite Happy and Author of *Live Your Possible*

"Brian's wisdom and genuine leadership shine through every chapter of *Corporate Campfire Stories*, where each narrative is crafted with intention and resonance. These stories, both relevant and relatable, serve as bridges between the realms of work and life, revealing that the lessons we glean in one sphere inevitably enrich the other. With deliberate curation, every story becomes a testament to the seamless interplay between professional growth and personal fulfillment—reminding us that to nurture one is to elevate both. I highly recommend *Corporate Campfire Stories* to everyone! Brian's lessons apply wherever you are on your career journey."

—Diane Lopes
Continuous Improvement Leader, Arch Capital

"If I only had this book when I was starting out! This is no-nonsense advice for everyone, designed to take you on an informative journey leading to an incredible and more satisfying professional career."

—Adam Hallet
President and Owner, Hallet Enterprise

"*Corporate Campfire Stories* speaks directly to the heart of leadership through wisdom earned from adversity and serendipitous turns. Each story resonates with my own journey, revealing how homophily—our shared humanity—and connections sustain us through change. These hard-won lessons kindle the passion to lead with empathy and purpose, reminding us that growth comes from the stories we gather along the way."

—Tracy Ann Shaw, Ph.D.
Head of Engagement Strategy, Equitable

Corporate Campfire Stories

Corporate Campfire Stories

A Practical Career Guide for Aspiring Leaders

BRIAN HAENDIGES

Publish Your Purpose
141 Weston Street, #155
Hartford, CT, 06141

The opinions expressed by the Author are not necessarily those held by Publish Your Purpose.

Ordering Information: Quantity sales and special discounts are available on quantity purchases by corporations, associations, and others. For details, contact the author at CorporateCampfireStories@proton.me.

Edited by: Anna Heim, Nancy Graham-Tillman, Lily Capstick
Cover design by: Mark Pate
Lantern graphic by Moriym Begum at Vecteezy.com
Typeset by: Medlar Publishing Solutions Pvt Ltd., India

ISBN: 979-8-88797-214-5 (hardcover)
ISBN: 979-8-88797-215-2 (paperback)
ISBN: 979-8-88797-216-9 (ebook)

Library of Congress Control Number: 2025924353

First edition, March 2026.

Publish Your Purpose is a hybrid publisher of non-fiction books. Our mission is to elevate the voices often excluded from traditional publishing. We intentionally seek out authors and storytellers with diverse backgrounds, life experiences, and unique perspectives to publish books that will make an impact in the world. Do you have a book idea you would like us to consider publishing? Please visit PublishYourPurpose.com for more information.

*A portion of the profit from this book
will be donated to organizations helping
young people thrive and succeed by
acquiring learning and skill.*

Contents

Part 3: Wing to Wing

Foreword

When I first met Brian Haendiges, I didn't know him and I didn't want to.

Brian and I met in two dimensions, one on a screen during a global pandemic, and the other through a major organizational change during a corporate transition. The dimensions of complexity in my life at the time were multifaceted both personally and professionally. Personally I was grieving the loss of a child, and professionally I was at the crossroads of quiet ambition and quiet frustration.

Brian was sent to do a job, not dissimilar to the experience in Jacksonville, Florida, he shares in the introduction. (It's astounding how many times he has been "The Fixer.") He was the new business CEO, and I was somewhere in the middle, working hard, thinking deeply, but not yet seen. Our interactions were grounded solely in a shared commitment to the future of the business.

But something shifted. Slowly at first, then as if all at once.

I would say that Brian saw me, but he didn't just see me, he let me see him.

Brian's leadership was marked by a rare blend of strategic rigor and emotional intelligence. He could dissect a financial model with precision and then pivot to a conversation about employee morale with equal fluency. He understood that numbers tell a story, but people live it.

The narratives in *Corporate Campfire Stories* aren't just about business but about humanity. The ones I remember most are about Brian's family. Those are the ones in which you see his heart; the ones that make you laugh, smile, and cry; the ones that don't have a corporate moral but a human one. And that, at the end of the day, is what matters. When the fire burns out, what's left are the stories that warm, those that ignite something in someone else.

I would say that Brian saw me, but he didn't just see me, he finished me.

At his retirement party, our company CEO had a slip of the tongue and said that through his mentorship and succession planning, Brian had "finished Jamala off." There was lots of laughter from the packed ballroom of well-wishers, but in a lot of ways that wasn't a slip; it was the truth. Before meeting Brian, the idea of me being a CEO wasn't on my radar (nor anyone else's). The lessons I learned from him shaped me into what I needed, not to be perfectly ready—because there's no such thing—but to be prepared. And preparation, as I've come to learn, is part of the foundation of leadership.

One of the most memorable moments in our collaboration was our leadership transition itself. It was not a handoff but a hand-up. Brian didn't just pass the baton; he lifted the team, the culture, and the vision to a place where continuity felt natural and progress felt inevitable. His message to the organization, called "The Past, The Present & The Future," was more than a farewell. Brian reminded us that legacy is not what you leave behind but what you leave within. It was a blueprint for enduring leadership, and for this book.

The magic of this book is that you will feel that Brian sees you, too. That's the thing about the gift of stories—we find ourselves in them. We find ourselves in the moments of courage, vulnerability, and hard truths, and that's what you'll find here—not a secret roadmap but a series of moments, conversations, challenges, encouragements, and reckonings, the moments that shape our own stories, stories that become values, values that become legacy.

In today's corporate world, we've seen a trend toward fireside chats, meaning leaders are speaking more candidly, vulnerably, and authentically. Brian was doing that before it was trendy. He didn't need a stage or a spotlight, he just needed a moment, a hallway conversation, a quiet check-in, or a well-timed challenge to trigger a spark.

Writing this foreword is not just a professional courtesy. It's a way of honoring the fire Brian built, the kind that leaves glowing embers that start another fire and continue forever in the ISBN of leadership, legacy, and culture on these pages.

To those reading this, I invite you to see these stories as possibilities—possibility to be the type of person who leads with empathy, not ego; possibility to be the type of leader who mentors, not manages; possibility to be the type of mentor who prepares others for responsibility, not just to fill a role. I invite you to let these stories inspire you to build your own fire, knowing that someone else may be warmed by its glow.

Thank you, Brian, a.k.a. The Fixer, The Finisher, The Friend. Thank you for your stories.

Jamala Arland
Business CEO

Introduction

Retiring from a long career in financial services and insurance shocked me. It wasn't that I hadn't planned for it but that I found out how much I didn't know about it. I learned so many new things that I've since taught a class on retirement topics to groups of emerging seniors at a local community college.

Retirement is also one of those milestones that trigger reflection, whether on your life so far, on just how different things are going to be, and especially on your career. How did I get here? What lessons did I learn? What worked and what didn't? The answers are the product of several past moments of decision-making, some that worked out well and others that didn't. You may well be facing decision points right now in your own career, no matter what stage you're in:

- How should I get my career off the ground?
- What's my next step?
- How do I get recognized for what I'm bringing to the table?
- How do I solve a complex problem?
- How do I get through to this person, this team, this organization?
- How do I get better?
- Is this decision worth the risk?

- What do I do now that I've been laid off?
- How do I fix something that's broken?
- How do I deal with a challenge?
- Should I raise the price I'm offering? Lower it? Keep it the same?

This book is designed to help you figure out how to answer questions like these so that you can supplement your own experience with that of others and better negotiate not only a career in corporate America but the decisions that come with it.

How Many People Are You Here to Fire, and Who Are They?

I'm sitting across the table from my new senior leadership team, who have just asked the above question. They're glaring at me with a mix of distrust, skepticism, anticipation, and impatience.

I've just made the first commute between a home in Connecticut and a new work role in Jacksonville, Florida, a route that eventually grew so familiar that once, as I was being seated in a TGI Fridays in Atlanta's Hartsfield-Jackson International Airport, the busiest in the US, I was greeted with a "Welcome back, Mr. H.," even though I'd submitted my name at the desk as "Brian."

Accompanied by one of our best HR folks, one who's recognized for helping teams put their issues on the table to resolve difficult situations, we're engaged in an "accelerated assimilation," a single-day approach intended to familiarize ourselves with each other so we can get off on the right foot. I've started with a quick overview of my background and a few comments about why we're here and what we hope to get done today, and I've listened to each of them provide their own summaries of background and what they do.

After an 8 a.m. start, I've stepped out for what was meant to be an hour or two while they're compiling a list of questions for me to answer when I return. When I finally reconvene with them after lunch, their list isn't the ten or twenty questions expected. It's eighty. And that one about people losing their jobs is only the first.

There's a reason for the team's animosity. They've been through six mergers, acquisitions, and layoffs in the prior five years. They're 1,100 miles away from and feel neglected by the rest of the organization, and the divide is more than distance alone. It feels cultural. They've been corrected countless times on their pronunciation of Quincy, Massachusetts, the distant city in which headquarters is based. Mutual trust has completely eroded.

Yet that's the *relationship* problem. The *business* problem is a far bigger mess than I've been led to believe.

The team's job is to calculate how much an employee is due from their pension when they retire, then cut them checks. Sounds pretty simple. It's not. The data is often distributed among multiple systems, which often disagree. Formats range from computer files to old photocopies kept in a basement cabinet somewhere. Calculations are complex and unclear, often conflicting due to multiple corporate mergers and divestitures of the companies that employed these new retirees. The knowledge of how complicated formulas interact is diminishing, as those who know the history, both for us and for our customers, are aging out of the workforce and cashing in their pensions themselves.

The worst part is how long it's taking for retirees to be paid. One of our customers, a name-brand manufacturer of T-shirts and underwear, told me at our introductory meeting that if their retiring employees have to wait more than two weeks for their first retirement paycheck, they have to rely on friends, neighbors, and local churches just to eat.

If we took the volume of work and spread it among our employees, our backlog would stretch those two weeks to eighteen months! We're having our people work lots of overtime, we're paying contractors exorbitant rates two to three times what we pay non-overtime employees, and we've redirected folks from their main jobs (such as IT) to getting checks out, yet we're still running months behind.

Oh, and we're losing money.

To top it off, I'm not here by choice. As a result of a meeting with HR to find places for my innovation team who were being disbanded in a downsizing effort following the 2008 global financial crisis, I found out from a friend that I was to be laid off myself, unless I could shop around within the company to find a different job by the end of the month. Leveraging an old relationship with a senior leader, I found a role heading up our defined benefit administration business. Still living in Connecticut and commuting to Florida, I had to learn another new business and how to fix it. It was a personal challenge as well as a business one.

I had always headed businesses that were driven by numbers—improve sales, earnings, retention, margins. This was a purely operational processing arena, an area in which I had no experience other than theory. I initially faced three significant career-defining challenges, each in a category representative of one you're likely to encounter as you navigate your own path:

1. I had no experience in the new area I was managing, particularly running an operations function.
2. I had multiple people-related issues, with skepticism and lack of engagement being among the most challenging.
3. I had a pressing business problem: an eighteen-month backlog coupled with negative earnings.

These challenges, in essence, are what this book is designed to address. We all want to improve and achieve success in our careers, but the path to growth isn't always straightforward. In this book, I share the lessons I've learned about solving complex problems in a corporate environment, taking risks, and developing skills. I also provide advice on motivating individuals and teams, including peers and hierarchical superiors because they're vital to growth. Finally, I demonstrate how your success and the success of the organization you work within are closely linked, with practical tips on making your organization (and yourself) better in the process. If you keep reading, you'll see how these principles played out in my own experience, including the obstacles I faced in Florida.

Why This Book?

There are hundreds, probably thousands of books prescribing how to do better at work. Why bother with one more? What most caught my attention about these other books were two common deficits:

1. As a visiting lecturer, I once left a group of eager MBAs and their professor in shock by starting a class with, "If you expect to hear from me how to become the next CEO of a company, I'm going to disappoint you." There's a lot of advice geared toward top-level executives, and I wanted to give them practical guidance instead. While I expect much of the advice included here is useful at all levels, whether you're just starting out, are mid-career, or have risen to be a leader in charge of thousands of people, many of the stories included here are intended for those of us in the middle of the journey, those trying to figure out every day how to make better decisions, manage people,

deal with obstacles, and get better at what we do. Most of us never reach the C-suite, yet we still yearn for a successful career and to enjoy at least the third to half of our waking hours we spend working.

2. Many other books are highly theoretical. To add to Yogi Berra's famous advice, you can observe a lot by watching, but you can also learn a lot by doing. Experiences matter, and not just those that result in success. Mistakes are great teachers. I once had a karate instructor who said that his best tool for teaching students not to overextend their front kick was to practice it while facing a wall. You bruise or break your toes once, and you don't do it again. I learned.

The more things you can do for yourself, the more you can retain. While the anecdotes and stories in this book aren't yours, I've tried to bring them to life enough that you feel like you were there, experiencing a loss with me or celebrating a success.

Why Stories and Anecdotes?

Simply put, we remember stories much more than we do facts.

I've always loved listening to stories, and I usually go back and forth between half a dozen audiobooks, three or four on paper, and a handful of television series all at the same time.

Stories are fascinating.

Initially an introvert, I've found out that I enjoy telling them. With several short stories written, two novels in the works, and a few more in the queue, I've got a lot to say on this topic. A good story is remembered, particularly by those who feel a connection to it. Take this example for instance.

I had parked my car in the visitors' lot of a company I formerly worked for and was walking toward the building for a friend's retirement party when someone rushed out of the building and ran toward me. I thought I was about to get a lecture about parking in the wrong spot without a proper hangtag. I didn't. He recognized me and wanted to let me know that the lessons he'd applied from a story I'd told him had changed his career, gotten him promoted, and made him happier at work. While to this day I don't know which story it was, it was important and memorable to him.

There's something Darwinian about stories, and I don't just mean that struggle for survival and growth against an antagonist or difficult odds that's inherent in any good story. The stories that survive are the ones that are more interesting, whether it's Odysseus running an endless life-and-death obstacle course to return home or Andy Dufresne crawling out of Shawshank Prison.

The birth of a child is a miracle, often the most important day in someone's life when asked. But for the nurses who do it every day, maybe it's not that memorable. When my second grandchild was born, he left a lifelong memory for his parents, but he also gave the nurses a story they could tell over dinner that evening.

My daughter-in-law, who's very organized and had a go bag already packed weeks before, told our son it was time to go to the hospital. They made their way out to the car, and that's as far as they got. She leaned over the hood of the Toyota and said, "The baby's coming."

"I know. That's why we're on the way to the hospital," my son said.

"No! The baby's coming now!"

My son ran into the house, washed his hands, and returned just in time to use his soccer goalkeeper skills to catch the baby and hand him to his mom.

By the time the EMTs arrived, the doula had already walked them through immediate care by phone, and the new mom and baby were resting. Mom walked calmly to the ambulance while the new dad jumped around like an excited puppy and asked what he could do to help. He followed the ambulance to the hospital, calling an at-first-unbelieving new grandpa on the way.

A line of excited nurses performed the equivalent of a slow clap at the end of a 1980s movie, pointing, whispering, and elbowing each other as the trio made their way down the hall to their room. "That's them," they said. "The baby was born in the garage."

We remember the unusual, the unexpected, the struggle, the pictures with enough detail to stand out later.

That's why stories. We connect to them, and we remember them.

Why Should You Listen to Me?

A question you might be asking is why you ought to pay any attention to someone who's retired after spending over forty years in medium and large corporations. How can that experience be relevant to someone who's younger and navigating a world full of constantly changing new technology, start-ups, and different cultures?

First, I focus on stories that reflect the dynamics inherent to human relationships as we get together in groups. Technology may advance, office floor plans change or even have us working from home, and headlines may differ, but certain core interactions remain fundamentally the same.

Second, medium and large corporations continue to exist and likely will for a long time. Other new medium and large companies might replace them, but they persist. And I've worked in them not just at multiple levels but across all aspects of an organization, from innovation, new product development, marketing, pricing, and sales on the front end to product management, client retention, and process improvement of existing books of business. I've run operational areas, an investment shop, and functional staff teams, and I've engineered new growth, improved existing businesses, and worked out of businesses that were past their prime.

But the third and most important reason hit me at the end of a class I was guest lecturing for in Virginia: "That was a master class in navigating a company."

"Thank you."

"I took lots of notes, but you should write some of those stories down. Other people will want to see them."

What Constitutes Success?

Defining success is harder than you might think.

One of the things that enabled me to retire with a clear conscience was having a very capable and motivated successor and team. About a year before my successor took over, we were having a work catch-up conversation over dinner, and she asked how I defined success. It took me aback, but after a moment of introspection I explained: "When I first started out, success was doing the impossible. If you wanted to motivate me, tell me no one had figured out how to do it before or that it was going to be too hard."

She nodded with a glint of curiosity, or perhaps skepticism.

"Then when I was well along in my career, I still wanted to defy expectations but on a broader scale. Give me a new business to grow or one that needs a turnaround, and I'll grow it or fix it."

Same nod, less glint.

"Now I'm old enough and close enough to retirement that success is seeing others grow, get better, and realize what they're capable of. Most importantly, I live for that moment when someone realizes just how good they are at what they do."

At that, the skepticism disappeared and the conversation started for real.

My point is twofold: (1) My definition of success changed over time, and (2) as I changed, the environment around me changed. Heraclitus is known to have philosophized about no one ever stepping into the same river twice. As with defining success, it's rarely the same river or the same person.

While you'll find nuggets of advice throughout this book, here's one I'll provide right up front. Think about it right now, before you get started: How do *you* define success? What's most important to *you*? The answer doesn't have to be perfect, and you can always change it as you go, but having a starting point allows you to know what you're looking for as you read and move ahead.

How to Read This Book

You can read this book in any order. It does present topics by category, and there are a few stories that reference others, but you should be able to pick up the gist no matter what order you ingest it. I do hope you'll read all of it.

If you're one of those people who likes things boiled down, there's a nice summary roadmap at the end, though you'll miss the reinforcing stories if you jump there.

Enjoy, and please share your own stories with others. Ask for theirs too so that you can all learn and grow.

Have fun!

Finding, Planning, and Managing a Career

I often felt my career was a series of events that happened to me, landing me in particular jobs as a result of good and bad luck. But as the old saying goes, "Luck favors the prepared mind." If you can get an early sense of what makes you tick, what drives and fulfills you, what you're good at and therefore have the potential to be excellent at, you can increase your chance of being lucky, of finding and shaping the career you want to have. That's what this section covers: finding and creating a positive career environment, choosing a career, learning from everything around you in the early days, and shaping the career and reputation you desire.

- Chapter 1 confirms the importance of continual learning and provides some tips on how to get and stay motivated to learn.
- Chapter 2 takes you through finding that first job and learning from it.
- Chapter 3 helps you optimize what you get out of those early job experiences.
- Chapter 4 covers building, maintaining, and optimizing relationships.
- Chapter 5 is about managing your career to maintain the right direction and growth.

Live and Learn

We learn throughout our lives, from the moment we're babies and first recognize a face or a voice to finding a career, partner, and place to live; from rising through the ranks at a job to dealing with setbacks and celebrating promotions; and from raising kids and retiring to losing those close to us and facing our own mortality.

In a career in particular, learning is a measure of accomplishment and progress. I once sat with every one of eighty new employees to ask each one individually what was most important to them in their jobs, and what I heard back from all but two was that they wanted to have an impact and to continue to learn. What motivates us to learn can drive our future direction in life, in particular for a career.

In this chapter, we'll cover the following questions:

- *What inspires us to learn?*
- *In what situations do we learn best?*
- *How can we learn from the things that don't go well?*
- *If I want to learn and get better at the job, what should I look for?*

Ouch! That's Hot!

My lab partner and I are sitting in an eighth-grade introductory class to integrated study of the physical sciences. We're performing an experiment called "distillation of wood," meaning burning some wood and then collecting the component parts of residue through a setup of burners, tubes, and beakers in what looks like Dr. Frankenstein's laboratory. We're supposed to test the resulting liquids that fall into the various beakers for different things such as color, cloudiness, or viscosity, though we're wisely advised not to taste any of them. We suddenly land on a brilliant idea.

"You know, maybe we should test flammability."

"Yeah!"

We grab a paper towel, soak it in the liquid, and light it. Whoosh! The flames reach almost to the suspended ceiling, our eyelashes curl from the heat, and the instructor takes only seconds to spray us and our desk with foam to put out the fire. He looks at us with a kind of "What was that all about?" expression, somewhat upset but I think more bemused.

We're still shaking, but we turn to each other laughing. "Flammable. Check."

Likely one of the reasons you're reading this book is to learn something. There are lots of ways to do it, and they don't all have to involve conflagration or the risk of imminent demise.

I have a further admission beyond almost blowing up a science lab: I love to learn. Not always in the moment, though. A tough performance review at work, turning around a business in trouble, having an argument with a significant other, stalling out a car's manual transmission at a light on a hill, touching a hot stove, or getting a punch in the mouth can all be learning experiences, but they're not necessarily fun, and they can even lead to discouraging us from wanting to learn further. So what exactly *does* make us want to figure things out?

Think that through in your own life. What makes you want to learn more? How can you tap into that to encourage yourself to improve, even when some of the lessons are hard?

Here's some background on my own path to learning. Perhaps you'll find some parallels.

More Syrup, Please

Some of the best learning (I would argue most of it) happens outside a classroom, but for a lot of us a classroom is where formal learning starts, and it's often accompanied by structure.

From the very beginning, I've had trouble with rules, so one of my first dislikes in school was penmanship. We learned cursive using the "Palmer Method," which was extra confusing for first and second graders like me who lived in Palmer, Massachusetts. It wasn't logical; it was just rules. "Write this part of the letter above the line and this part below," and "A Capital Z has to have just the right-sized loop in it."

Part of the challenge was that I wasn't very good at penmanship compared with other subjects. For math, my dad worked with me at the kitchen table before I ever went into first grade (there was no public kindergarten in town, and my folks couldn't afford private school). He'd ask, "How many apples are over here on this side of the table?"

"Three."

"On this side?"

"Two."

"So, how many all together?"

"Five."

Then the same thing with pennies, nuts, or washers.

One day he asked, "What if I have two piles of x's?"

"What's an x?"

"Could be anything. A box but you don't know what's inside it, pennies, nuts, apples, or something else."

"Oh. Five x's then."

So, yeah. Algebra before elementary school. Math was easy, penmanship was hard, and I was frustrated even after the success of working up my grade from a C to a B.

There it was, an early observation about learning, and many years later it carried into motivating both myself and others.

> *People are motivated by what they like and what they realize they're good at.*

A Little Longer Leash

Those of you who were kids when I was will remember a reading library in the back of the classroom, usually next to the monster-sized paper cutter that one comedian describes as capable of beheading a bull, where there were stories on cards. The easy stories were on glossy cards sporting bright colors such as red, blue, or yellow, and the harder stories were on black, brown, or gray cards. You'd read the story, answer some questions on the back, and based on your score you either repeated the section until you got it right or you moved on to the next. Each student worked at their own pace, and most enjoyed it.

And that led to another takeaway.

> **People are motivated by the acquisition of skills, specifically when they can control and see their progress.**

Learning for Dummies

One of my least favorite high school classes was American history, which was prosecuted by a hard-nosed battle-ax with strict rules and exacting definitions, and maybe a bit of showing off.

When a student once called another "stupid," rather than hearing a simple "That's not a nice name to call someone. Don't do it," we endured a forty-five-minute lecture on the difference between a moron, an imbecile, and an idiot on the Stanford-Binet IQ test. It had nothing to do with class. It was just her chance to express a strong opinion to a captive audience.

In a paper I wrote with my colleague Deb Dupont on behavioral connections to financial decisions, she came across a piece of research on Malcolm Knowles, the father of andragogy, the adult learning equivalent of pedagogy. One of his five principles of adult learning is that people want to understand the "why" behind learning.

Even more so than a high schooler asking how they'll ever use geometry in real life, adults need a reason.

> **Learners seek relevance.**

Pete and Repeat Sat on a Fence

Somehow, I rotated among four or five different English classes, reading Longfellow's endless poem *Evangeline* in each one. It wasn't hard to pass a test I'd seen before, but what a waste. Then came *The Scarlet Letter* by Hawthorne. That and his *House of the Seven Gables* have to be two of the driest books ever written, so much so that the former is the only book I ever got CliffsNotes for so that I didn't have to read the original. Every chapter seemed to repeat the same points.

In my sitting down with hundreds of people in performance and career discussions over the years, one thing that came up frequently was that they really didn't want to keep doing the same thing again and again.

There's a corollary to relevance.

 **_Many learners seek variety._** 

You Can't Do That

On the other side of the equation (pun slightly intended), math class was fun, in part because it felt natural and also because it could be challenging.

One day, our geometry teacher told the class that no one, not even Euclid, had discovered a way to trisect an angle using traditional methods. I worked the problem for two weeks, taking as a win that it could be done but only for certain angles and conditions.

In Algebra II, Mr. H. mentioned a "higher level problem too advanced for a high school class": to find the square root of 1 + i, where i is the imaginary number, the square root of negative 1. I was excited to bring him the solution the next day.

> ***Although many of us are initially intimidated by a challenge, true learning takes place when we overcome one.***

Hacking and Matching Wits

Algebra wasn't the only valuable experience I had with Mr. H. The first was that the school had received this new thing called a computer, which no one at the school knew how to use. As a math teacher who liked trying new things, Mr. H. took on the task of learning how to program it, and he selected four students to help him figure it out. We shared a battered manual for the computer language BASIC, coaxing output during study hall from a giant reel-to-reel tape drive and a chain-link printer that hammered away like a stock ticker.

Unknowingly emulating the culture described in the book *Hackers*, a history of the playful doings and ethos of the early days of computing that grew out of the MIT model railroad club, we played a "hack," or little joke, on our teacher by simulating his login screen with a program that played the high school marching band's drumbeat on that noisy printer.

Mr. H. also escorted me, zigging and zagging through traffic in his beat-up old teacher's car, to a meeting with a future employer, MassMutual, where I encountered two lasting impressions. One was a robotic mail cart that even in 1977 followed a chemical scent track on the floor, periodically stopping to let people take out or put in daily interoffice memos. The other was sitting in an executive's office that felt like the size of a football field while hearing how I really ought to pursue an actuarial career. Over thirty years later, I had many meetings with MassMutual's chief actuary in that same office, and the company used the same yellow envelopes for mail, though the automated cart had disappeared by then, having been replaced, regressively, by a human.

Mrs. O., who taught calculus through a rigorous but hint-laden figure-it-out-yourself approach, also coached our team for "As Schools Match Wits," a *Jeopardy!*-style quiz show that pitted local high schools against each other. I think we lost every year, but we enjoyed ourselves. We were being badly out-answered by a studious and primly dressed larger school when we received the question, "What happened on April 14, 1865?"

Instead of a poised, professional answer provided in a deep, authoritative, and appropriately somber newscaster voice, perhaps something like "President Lincoln was assassinated," and seeing that we finally had a question we knew the answer to, we yelled out as one: "Lincoln got shot! Lincoln got shot!" We celebrated wildly, with whatever was the equivalent of the high five.

 **_Camaraderie, competition, and fun can be great tools to enhance learning._** 

In the Lab

Math and science are closely related, and I liked some science courses for a lot of the same reasons I liked math, but maybe more because of teaching style and enthusiasm. Chemistry, biology, and anatomy were tedious, including measuring exactly, documenting appropriately, and putting things into precise categories. Once again, following the rules. By contrast, the distillation of wood class was hands-on and, even with flash fires, was a lot of fun as a result. You could see what you were learning.

Our physics teacher was brilliant but very laid back. He let his students try out different things, including measuring how much easier we could make lifting something by using pulleys. That had practical applications in real life. Another experiment measured how fast a ball rolled down a hill at different angles. He helped us borrow a clock from the gym teacher, and we took it apart and hooked it up to electrodes to run trials. We then took the results to the basement computer lab, plugged them in, and graphed them. Voilà! A perfect sine curve.

It's moments of insight and revelation like that one that bring you back to learning again and again. Malcolm Knowles agrees with this in another of his principles of andragogy. We become more self-directed as we mature. We also remember things better when we learn them on our own.

 *Learning by doing makes learning better and longer lasting.* 

You Can Do This the Easy Way
or the Hard Way

Let me go to one other category, embodied by two totally different styles, but both of which were motivating.

Mrs. M., whom I much admired, taught both English rhetoric and Latin, and both could be brutal. A student might walk into class to find the short essay they'd written that week projected on a screen and then cringe in their seats as she tore it apart until it had more of her red corrections on it than their original writing. It made us wish for a hot stovetop to put our hands on instead, but we learned, and we remembered! (For the record, it's "just between you and me" not "just between you and I," and the last syllable of "connoisseur" is pronounced "sir," because who wants to associate elegance with a sewer?)

Another English class was an entirely different experience. In Gothic Literature, we read and talked about *Frankenstein*, *Dracula*, and other horror. The subject matter was intriguing, but the real fun for me derived from the admittedly selfish approach of the teacher. He'd have a traditional class or two at the beginning of the week, and the rest of the week he'd send everybody to the library to do "research" on that week's report. When they all left, he'd direct me to "Go get out the board." I'd teach him chess, and he actually improved his rating significantly. It was fun to be valued for knowledge I had that he didn't, and to reciprocate the joy of learning.

 *An important component of good learning is the relationship with the teacher.* 

Rah!

One more from school.

Our guidance counselor, Mr. N., a mid-range chess player himself, ran a club for students where he'd show us a concept and then let us try it out at our own levels. In this way, he created a number of players better than he was, a remarkable accomplishment.

He was gentle with his remonstrations and excited for us when we figured something out. When I drew (tied) against the New England champion, he posted the winning scoresheet in his office.

> *It's good to have a fan and cheerleader.*
> *We relish encouragement as we learn.*

Encounters with the Real World

Learning and motivation take on more shape when you transition from an academic environment to real-world application.

I had unpaid chores growing up, some assigned and some that seemed to appear without warning. I enjoyed occasional tasks for a dime or a quarter, but my first job with an agreed-upon wage was when I was fourteen and helped my dad build a garage from the ground up, in the shape of a barn. Together, we surveyed the plot with borrowed equipment, laid out the foundation, and dug the hole for it by hand. We removed or buried gargantuan rocks using an old 2 x 12 and a couple of metal pry bars, mixed and poured a footing, and built a foundation wall out of masonry blocks.

We had outside help on only two tasks, pouring the concrete floor and lifting the center beam and walls, which we'd framed in advance. We were on our own to install torsion braces, floor and ceiling beams, flooring, plywood walls, rafters (I got to use some of that trigonometry), a roof (including tar paper and shingles), doors, windows, vents, trim work, a drop-down ladder, shake shingles for siding, and two coats of paint.

My wage was minimal, but it was a wage, and my dad didn't have to pay me. Work was expected. But he wanted me to get used to the idea of being responsible, doing a good job, and being rewarded for it.

> *When learning becomes tangible and visible, a spark ignites.*

Not Just Sawed Liver

More important than the paycheck was acquiring new skills. I didn't go into carpentry, but I was motivated to find out that you can learn new things even if you know nothing about them at the start. I also discovered I could solve unexpected problems, such as how to cut a rafter for a gambrel roof and the most efficient way to cut 4 x 8 sheets of plywood to cover a floor.

When I became legally old enough to work, Dad hinted he could finish the barn on his own by directing me to go get a "real" job. I found one with the local supermarket, where one of our church deacons was manager or part-owner. That first job was cleaning the meat room, working for two long-tenured meat cutters who each got a week of vacation a year, one of whom was about to upgrade to two weeks after twenty years of service.

I started with an initiation. My first task was to clean up the mess from a large container of corned beef that had gone bad. The more senior of the butchers introduced me to the chore with a bit of philosophy: "There are two kinds of workers in the world: fast and half-assed. Let's see which one you are." I must have passed, because they kept me on.

The day-to-day work was challenging. Besides keeping the refrigerator clean, laying down sawdust, breaking down boxes, ruining pants by bleaching the cutting tables, and cleaning the restroom until it was spotless (but only after all of the other cleaning), I also had the job of cleaning the band saw. Mondays were "breakdown days," which were the worst. The butchers sliced up big sides of beef into smaller pieces, and though I could usually get the saw clean in about half an hour, when they'd get a delivery of liver it took forever to get it out of the nooks and crannies.

Still, just as with swinging a hammer, there was acquisition of skills. I can still fold a band saw. To this day, though, I do not like corned beef, even on St. Patrick's Day, or liver.

> ***Once again, there is pride and reinforcement in the acquisition of skills.***

Po-tay-toes

Other part-time high school jobs taught similar lessons.

Washing dishes at a local country club made even a teen's back ache by the end of the night, but that paled in comparison to pots-and-pans duty, or worse, emptying "the pig," the catch basin into which all of the leftovers from diners' plates fell or were rinsed off. Usually, this garbage weighed so much we needed two people to carry it downstairs and lift its contents into a dumpster.

Holidays, however, were even worse. On New Year's Eve, the glasses piled up, and we had to do everything we could to keep up with them, including letting the plates stay dirty until later. For Thanksgiving, we received four hundred pounds of potatoes, put down broken-up cardboard boxes on the floor of the storage room, sat in a circle on overturned five-gallon buckets, and peeled until we could barely see over the pile in the center of the floor. After dinner was served the next day, we had to debone about twenty turkeys.

There was good camaraderie with the work, and quite a bit of joking. Often we were excited when someone complained about how their food was cooked and sent it back. On the unusual occasion when a steak was returned, four forks might stab toward the plate at once.

Pride, this time, came from slotting nine plates with one hand into a dishwasher tray and from peeling potatoes faster than anyone else.

 **_Learning with others enhances the experience._** 

Necessity Is a Mother

I built stone walls with a friend named Danny. It was for a local jeweler, Irv, who paid us $1.90 an hour under the table, beneath the then-minimum wage of $2.10 but seemingly acceptable because there were no taxes deducted.

We mixed our own concrete (with sand and with lime, but not too much because it weakens the concrete), lined up the stones with a homemade plywood guide, and used gloved fingers dipped in water to smooth the work product.

Irv had only one leg, so he had manufactured some contraptions in a way he could work them. He had a combination front loader and backhoe for moving the stones, to which he rigged a piece of metal pipe to the clutch so he could operate it by hand. It worked like a charm once you got used to it.

> *Ingenuity can be a source of pride and*
> *a motivator to continue learning.*

Summary

Learning and motivation are closely connected. Whether you're motivating others to learn or motivating yourself, keep these things in mind:

- *People are motivated by what they like and what they realize they're good at.*
- *There's motivation, pride, and reinforcement in the acquisition of skills, especially when people can control and see their progress and apply their ingenuity.*
- *Learning improves with relevance and application as well as with variety, fun, camaraderie, and competition.*
- *Although many of us are initially intimidated by a challenge, true learning takes place when we overcome one.*
- *Learning by doing makes learning better and longer lasting.*
- *An important component of good learning is the relationship with the teacher.*
- *It's good to have a fan and cheerleader. We relish encouragement as we learn.*

- *Some of us learn more by seeing. When learning becomes tangible and visible, a spark ignites.*
- *Learning with others enhances the experience.*

Chapter 2

Off to a Good Start

Yes, there's a luck factor in landing a job or a promotion. However, if you've done a bit of introspection about what you like and don't like, you may just land in a good job from the start. We often don't, though. We have to accept what comes along. And either way, once we're in that job we have to try it on for size. Don't let this be a passive experience. Engage early and completely.

In this chapter, we'll cover the following questions:

- *What can I learn during the search for an initial job?*
- *Once I've started a new job, what should I emphasize to get the most out of it?*
- *How can I learn from every experience and person?*
- *How can I learn from mistakes?*

Luck, the Child of Diligence

"Show the upward force that the ground exerts on the building."

If this weren't an engineering school, I would've wondered whether I'd gone to the wrong class, maybe creative writing. As far as I knew, in this universe gravity works the other way around. Even in cartoons, Wile E. Coyote falls, albeit after a short wait during which he realizes he's stepped off a cliff.

The speaker was a professor of mechanical engineering, and the school was Worcester Polytechnic Institute (WPI), or "Whoopie-Tech" to some. I had landed in the class after a search for what I wanted to do and was now discovering that it was not mechanical engineering. Knowing what you're good at or interested in is one thing. Diving deeper and turning it into a career is something else entirely. I fell into the actuarial and insurance field seemingly by chance, though on closer inspection it was through some intentional narrowing of the field after some trial and error.

Based on my exposure to the burgeoning field of computers, I headed off to WPI thinking I'd be a programmer. I was soon disillusioned by a more restrictive environment and with having to submit punch cards to a grumpy and arrogant systems admin at 2 a.m., learn complex incomprehensible computer languages, and compete for terminal time with a yapping pack of wiry goateed experts who seemed to have built their own machines in their garages and been programming them since kindergarten.

Thinking there might be a correlation between mathematics and accounting, I tried my hand at that, but I found its rule-based systems confining and its concepts as inverted as those in mechanical engineering, only this time in the wrong columns instead of in backward arrows. "Debit" sounds like "debt," which is something you don't want so it should be a negative, but it wasn't. And "credit" sounds like a good thing, such as in the phrase "that's to your credit," so it should be a positive. Nope.

I thought there must be something in my long-standing infatuation with math, but even there I seemed to struggle. I once fell asleep in ring theory class, costing my buddy Leon five dollars when

I awoke perched on the back two legs of a chair with my head in the blackboard tray behind me and didn't fall, much to the disappointment of the crowd of thirty that had gathered to bet on me.

Just as with computers, I found some intensely smart mathematicians who amazed me. I was proud of myself for a presentation on something called "digital roots," which involves adding the digits of a number together. My jaw dropped when a classmate used arrays and matrices to design a missile guidance system that worked when faced with clouds or debris such as chaff in the air.

Surely there must be something with math that didn't involve statistical processing for manufacturing household appliances, or rockets.

Fortunately, upon approaching two years of school, I ran out of money. My folks had floated me a loan, and I'd also racked up student loans, yet I was bringing in a paltry few bucks through work-study. Having inadequate funds for the coming semester, I looked at something called a co-op program, which is when you graduate in five years instead of four but get two several-month-long stretches of work experience to spread out your expenses. There happened to be one available in mathematics, and, even better, if I could pass an upcoming actuarial exam it would come with a salary!

I worked with my advisor and faculty to create an independent major in actuarial science, solely for me. I sat for the first actuarial exam and passed it, which landed me a job in Wellesley Hills, Massachusetts, at Sun Life Assurance Company, a US sub of a Canadian parent company.

> ***Finding the first step in a career can be a combination of eliminating things that don't fit and exploring those you like.***

Shifting Gears

My learning in this new environment took place outside the office as well as at work, and it required creativity, networking, and a little horse trading.

First I needed a place to live. Working through the church network, I found a spare upstairs room that a divorcée was renting out to earn extra money, until she found a new man-friend and needed more privacy. Through the same network, I moved to lodge with a recent widower, for free if I'd do some cooking, yard work, and minor repairs (including some stone and cement work).

Transportation was another challenge. Without a car of my own, I borrowed a high-mileage, manual transmission Plymouth Valiant from my folks. Following one quick and mutually frustrating lesson with Dad, I managed to get the bucking vehicle to Wellesley. For the first few weeks, I stalled it multiple times at a light on a hill, until I found a longer but flatter way to work. I'd put five dollars of gas into the tank at a time and eventually got so comfortable with the standard that I bought one when I graduated. Even with stalling out and a gas tank on fumes, the independence was liberating.

The office component of the experience was invaluable.

The first benefit was all the people I met. There were actuarial students taking exams and deciding on their career direction, as well as full-fledged actuaries, notably Barry and Ron, and I got to see what they did every day. The two introduced me to my first assignment, programming a required disclosure document called a life insurance illustration, by getting me on a call with the company's top salesperson, who told me exactly what he needed to hit his sales target for the year. Yes it was intimidating, but it was also energizing. It had real-world impact.

Next I had to program the document in a new language called APL, the commands of which are a bunch of symbols that look like cuneiform. The difference from school, though, is that there were resources available to help, including a book, access to a terminal for as much time as I needed, other people who wrote similar code, and other people's prior work product to look at.

I struggled at first, leveraging code from another student who took great pride in the "elegance" of compressing programs into extraordinarily concise but nearly impenetrable steps. I started from scratch, checked with the agent to be sure it was what he needed, and got a very nice compliment from one of the other students about how readable and reusable the program was. I already felt useful.

Barry and Ron liked the results enough that I presented them to the divisional president and chief actuary, who had moved to the US from Canada to build, and later head, the US sub. He'd heard about the program when the sales team's results improved.

"I have one change I need you to make," he started, staring at me over his glasses with the intensity of someone who has interrogated thousands of people.

As I sat wondering what I'd done wrong, he explained.

"Please change the name of the sample insured from Jean Deaux back to John Doe." He then broke into a big grin and started laughing. "Well done," he said, then turned to Ron and Barry. "Watch this one. He's got a sense of humor."

Upon my departure, Ron and Barry called me into Ron's office, where they presented me with a $600 bonus, a seeming fortune at the time, along with an invitation to come back for another visit or for a job when I graduated.

I felt dually rewarded, first with a financial incentive to continue on the actuarial path, and second with the pride in having solved someone's problem in a creative way.

> ***When you're new to a job, tap into***
> ***the resources available and try stuff out.***

Back to School

I returned to campus and came upon a plan to cover the remaining tuition money.

WPI had a unique approach to its graduation requirements that was designed to build "technological humanists" at an engineering school. Students had to complete the equivalent of six semesters in the humanities, a project that related society and technology, another project in each student's major area of study, and a final competency exam overseen by a panel of professors and an outside industry expert.

Humanities culminated in a thesis written in German.

To relate society and technology, a classmate and I wrestled with the challenge of disciplining a group of gifted fourth graders as we taught them a college-level course. They were quite good at some challenging "fastest route" problems used in package delivery and telephone switching systems, but they were difficult to keep quiet and orderly.

To complete the project in our field of study, another actuarial student and I rewrote a pricing program for dental insurance for a local insurer. I found it still in use by the company twenty years later when I encountered our mentors as newly transferred employees at another company.

That left only the competency exam, considered by most students as the most demanding obstacle to graduation. As an example, on the first day engineer friends received problems such as, "Design a bridge from this building to that one" or "A one-liter pot of water is heated to boiling at a constant temperature of three hundred degrees Fahrenheit. Describe the airflow inside a 10 mm glass straw placed in the pot." Students then had seventy-two hours to solve the problem, during which they usually slept for only an hour or two, if at all, and then they presented their results to the supervisory panel for grading.

Actuarial students could forgo the entire grueling competency exam if they passed two or three actuarial exams, which I'd done on my co-op job with the help of the resources available. That got me out early and saved a year's worth of tuition.

I then worked with the office that helped students find jobs. Because of my unusual degree, they didn't have that many insurer contacts other than for sales jobs, but I managed some interviews at larger companies, both on campus and in Hartford, Connecticut, the insurance capital of the world. Because of WPI's unique non-letter grading system, I didn't even know what a GPA was when asked by a weary recruiter at one of the larger firms, who just made a note and went back to a tired pitch about how big his company was and how long they'd been in business. I landed in Maine with a smaller company called Union Mutual (now Unum), whose interviewer came in with a more human-centered pitch and an understanding of what an actuary does.

What sold me on a subsequent headquarters visit was, among other things, meeting a twenty-six-year-old who in 1981 was running a $600 million portfolio.

> *There's almost always a way to accomplish something, but only if you look for it.*

Roller Coaster Ride

My first full-time role was quoting interest rates on Guaranteed Interest Contracts (GICs), which are similar to bank CDs but are sold by insurers to institutional investors, typically retirement plans, with deals that back then ranged from $5 million to $50 million. I really enjoyed that level of responsibility, but I almost got canned my first week on the job when I quoted the wrong rate to the City of Detroit Police and Fire. I did a quick calculation and figured I'd just lost the equivalent of my salary on one deal.

Having hired me, my boss, Don, was disappointed in both of us, but he gave a gentle constructive correction: "Write the quote down first, then read it to the salesperson before sending the confirmation."

I followed his advice and never made the same mistake again.

It was a fast-paced environment. Quotes were generally good for twenty-four hours, and rates could move ten or twenty basis points (one hundredth of a percent) in a day, which was worth a lot of money. But that paled in comparison to one day in the summer of 1982 when rates moved by ten times that amount. To compound the issue, two of us had stayed behind after the rest of our colleagues left to make room for a scheduled building move, and the crew dismantled everything around us while we remained on the phone quoting rates to clients at a lone desk in the middle of an echoing space piled with debris. On a conference call with US Shoe regarding a $20 million deal, they asked how long the quote was valid given the day's crazy market. We responded with a chuckle and said, "Until this call is over," just as a crew member tripped over the phone cord, cutting off the connection.

Hearing a different phone ringing nearby with their frantic callback, I soon found myself picking up one phone after another from a massive pile, almost yelling "Hello? Hello? Hello?" until I finally made the connection and we did the deal. They didn't want to risk another disconnect.

I loved both the responsibility and impact I felt from the mistake made with Detroit, as well as the fast-paced environment of a deal in the making.

 *When you see something you like early in your career, remember it and look for more of it.* 

New Sheriff

One last story from those early days reinforced the lesson from Sun Life that dealing with a senior executive doesn't have to be intimidating.

Our new president and CEO, a former hockey star from Connecticut and much younger than his predecessor, joined the firm eager to make his mark, but he ran into a cultural challenge. At the time, the company prided itself on its open-door policy; even the prior president had worked in an open cubicle. In an attempt to maintain that policy while also retaining the opulent trappings of the bank, which he had left behind during his move to Maine, he set up a new executive office that indeed had no doors. However, it didn't go over so well with employees because the building was downtown, several miles away.

In a related stumble, the centerpiece of the new space was a substantial conference room that was to be adorned to impress the board with a jumbo-sized table cut from a single piece of Pacific Northwest timber and shipped carefully from Oregon with an "Oversized Load" warning. However, someone forgot to measure the office for it, and the delivery team had to cut it in half to get it through the doorway.

This was the same leader I encountered who tasked our division with providing break-even projections for a new 401(k) business, an assignment eventually passed down to me after several others insisted the effort had been tried before and discarded as impossible. I aimed to show not only a break-even year but the drivers behind it and the risks of achieving it, and I went about it with a simple approach: talking with people in each department and asking them questions. How much time did they spend on different tasks? And most importantly, What were their biggest problems? What did they worry about?

For a polished presentation, I used a third-party-operated color printer, a large new machine that required special pencils and hours of wait time. As the deadline approached, I kept getting printouts that were visually appealing but lacked clarity. The night before the presentation, I had a breakthrough insight. I flipped two variables and submitted the data. The next morning, the printout displayed not only a break-even projection but a perfect bell curve of cost per customer and driver.

Nervous about presenting to such a senior executive, I was relieved when the CEO praised the clarity of the analysis, calling it "the best, clearest, simplest explanation of profitability" he'd ever seen. That moment eased my nerves, especially when I caught him picking his nose during the presentation.

Years later, after I'd left, he shut down the underperforming business division when the desired drivers weren't achieved, both affirming the value of the exercise and boosting my confidence for future analyses.

Even high-level executives appreciate simplicity and clarity. They're also human.

Summary

The lessons learned early in a career can be just as crucial and lasting as those gained at more advanced stages. Remember this:

- *Be aware of what resonates with you and what doesn't, right from the beginning of searching for a career and even if you don't land exactly where you expect.*
- *Learn from every resource you can, and test yourself and your environment to see what you're capable of and attracted to.*
- *If you have one of those "Aha!" moments when you realize what you like, take a minute to pause and remember it.*
- *Every human audience values simplicity and clarity, both in processes and results.*
- *Be confident in a good work product and excited for the opportunity to present it.*

Chapter 3

Early Days

It's common to think of early job experiences on a spectrum. They can be opportunities to simply enjoy life outside work, some view it as the time to make their name known, and others seek that elusive work–life balance. Regardless, if we want to get the most out of our early experiences, it's worth throwing ourselves into them. Then, as we learn and grow, there are some specific skills we can rely on, not just early but throughout our careers, to learn and progress at an optimum level.

In this chapter, we'll cover the following questions, which especially apply early in a career or new role:

- *How do I face things I don't know or am afraid of?*
- *How do I know what to focus on?*
- *How do I make sure I'm not overwhelmed?*
- *How do I set reasonable objectives?*
- *How can I be sure to appreciate and absorb what I'm learning?*
- *How do I continue to invest in myself?*

Lessons from Larry

In the mid-1980s, I traveled to Los Angeles to fill in for a relationship manager who was out on maternity leave. Her boss, Larry, consistently the top sales manager in the country, engineered the trip, presumably so he'd have a pricing actuary in his pocket when asking for better rates. Though I remember the intimidation of prospecting and cold calling, what stands out are a couple of tidbits from a week of regional sales training.

"What do you think is the number one thing that correlates with high sales?" Larry started.

Answers ranged from how many calls we made to how we dressed and what haircuts we sported (we were in LA after all). He kept shaking his head to most of these answers, though he did acknowledge that keeping your promises, even small ones such as "I'll meet you at ten" or "I'll call back with an answer on Thursday," is important in building a relationship.

"Nope. The number one factor is your sense of confidence. You have to believe in what you're selling. Doesn't matter what it is, that's number one."

He then lectured about asking questions first rather than making an immediate sales pitch. "It's not about you. It's about what you can do for them." That lesson was passed on years later to my daughter, and it translated into her landing every job she's interviewed for.

Larry taught one other technique I've repeatedly seen used to good effect: "Suppose you know that you're up against a competitor and they have some clear advantages over your product that they're going to emphasize. What do you do?"

Again, a round of responses that didn't hit the mark.

"You acknowledge them. You tell the prospective client, 'Here's what you're going to hear from the other guy.' Then you tell them why that's wrong and why our product's better. When the competitor's salesperson gives their spiel, it reinforces that you were right. The more adamant they get, the more they're building you up."

Brilliantly simple.

> *Be confident. Be aware.*
> *Make it about them. Anticipate.*

People Like Me?

I had some fun opportunities to test Larry's lessons in confidence during the same trip. Working out of a long-term-stay apartment complex in the hills above Burbank Studios, I explored my new environment, starting with picking up a four-inch-thick pre-Google search tool called a phone book and looking for people who shared my surname. I found several, met one family at a local restaurant, displayed a Maine license for proof of identity, and was warmly welcomed into a new circle that included a plumber, an electrician, and a lawyer.

One evening, Disneyland roped off Tomorrowland for our private corporate event. I arrived at the entry gate with my company ID, two of my newfound and eager cousins, ages eight and ten, and no return transportation until the event's conclusion. A guard welcomed me in but initially refused admittance to the uninvited youngsters, until I asked him if he wanted the liability of us hanging out in the parking lot for four hours. An override from a supervisor and a company rep gained us admittance. Naive optimism, persistence, and Larry's lessons got us a dozen rides on Space Mountain with no lines, and later a pile of hamburgers and hot dogs.

The confident approach must have also translated into my physical demeanor. Most of the other tenants at the Burbank complex were aspiring actors and actresses with an ongoing comical interchange of how well they were doing, combined with trying to identify who else hanging out at the pool might be worth knowing. One turned to me after we'd just won a volleyball match and said he really liked the work I'd done "in that karate movie." Apparently I looked like someone.

 **Confidence can get you a long way.** 

Go Jump in the Lake

One special draw of LA was karate. Our style, Shotokan, came to the US in the 1950s with chief instructor Tsutomu Ohshima, who established the first nonprofit karate organization in the States. With LA as the national base, a variety of high-level instructors led classes at the local dojo, with Mr. Ohshima himself leading once a week. I took full advantage, getting to class as often as I could, including one Saturday morning for an expedition to an isolated canyon up the coast. One LA karate story stands out, and it starts with a dinner.

I'd been out with some of the Shotokan guys to try sushi for the first time. At first the idea of raw fish didn't appeal to me, but karate is about pushing beyond your comfort zones, and these guys lived by that ethos. Mr. Ohshima, who was connected to some of the top professionals in various fields, knew the best sushi chef in LA, a man who had once been the second-best in Japan. Sapporo beer and sake helped the night along.

But the night I'm recalling wasn't fancy like that one. My instructor from home, Marion, was in town for some event, and we were out for Friday beer and pizza, with work and practice already behind us. After about my third slice of pizza, Marion turned to me and asked, "Brian, what are you doing tomorrow?"

"Nothing. I'm just here for work."

"Glad to hear it. Here's what you're doing: You're going to Nisei Week." He explained the event is a celebration of the Nisei (second-generation Japanese Americans), held every year in LA and featuring Japanese food, music, and a karate tournament. My eyes lit up.

"Awesome! I'd love to watch some high-level karate," I said, thinking I'd get to observe the action.

"Oh, you're not going to be watching it. One of our East Coast team's fighters is sick. You're going to take his place."

You don't get a choice to bow out when Marion tells you you're doing something. The next morning, I found myself at the Nishi Hongwanji gymnasium in Little Tokyo, wearing my gi, surrounded by seasoned fighters from across the US and Canada, and listening to Mr. Ohshima introduce the other judges, including a special guest: the stuntman for Noriyuki "Pat" Morita, who portrayed Mr. Miyagi in the *Karate Kid* movies. I felt a rush of anxiety. I'd only recently earned my black belt, had sparred only a few times, and was now going up against some of the best. But I remembered something I'd heard when first starting out: "If you're afraid to get wet, go jump in a lake."

After seeing a short but clear bout in which one fighter dropped his flashy, whirling adversary with a single, simple jab, I faced two opponents: the Canadian champion and the previous year's US winner. I fought both with everything I had, walking away with a black eye from the Canadian and going the distance, but ultimately losing to the American by a wide margin.

Mr. Ohshima thanked me for stepping up and told me he almost gave me the "fighting spirit" award, but instead gave it to someone who made it further in the tournament. But he added, "Keep practicing." To me, this was the essence of karate and the journey I was on—constant self-improvement, no matter the immediate outcome.

George, one of Mr. Ohshima's first US students and a hard-nosed old-school instructor, led the few of us who made it to the following Monday's practice. Disappointed in the weekend's tournament and the inability of fighters to get past opponents' defenses, he led a grueling four-and-a-half-hour session that started with us facing the wall and practicing the last six inches of a punch and ended with intense sparring. As we worked through repetition, pushing our limits until we were exhausted and focusing on that crucial last bit of technique, his philosophy became clear: Only when you're tired enough to give everything you have can you truly begin to learn something new.

He closed the night with an uncannily accurate prediction: "Watch out for this boxing kid named Mike Tyson. He knows how to do what we've been working on tonight. He'll be world champion."

The entire experience, from Friday's pizza to Monday's prediction, was about embracing discomfort and pushing through it, about not backing down when faced with challenges no matter how intimidating they may seem. In the tournament, I'd stepped onto the floor with seasoned fighters, and though I lost both matches, I walked away with invaluable lessons in resilience and perseverance. As Mr. Ohshima had said, I needed to keep practicing.

The same applies to life. Constant self-improvement is key, and every challenge is an opportunity to learn and grow. That was the true lesson of the tournament, one that stuck with me long after my black eye healed.

 **_When faced with a new experience or challenge, throw yourself into it._** 

Behind the Sword

In retrospect, I'd already experienced this lesson in commitment, but I just didn't realize it until I attended Nisei Week.

Picture this: The cavernous gym echoes at night as prospective candidates for a black belt huddle around our senior instructor and half a dozen of his fiercest fighters. We're about to experience the "Gates of Heaven" practice in preparation for a test in a few days, if we're fortunate enough to be invited to take it. We lean in to listen.

"Hell is in front of the sword. Heaven is behind the sword."

This is the key. Each senior will attack us in turn. Our job is to let that attack proceed until the absolute last second and then, rather than back up defensively, penetrate in past the attacker to come out the other side behind him.

The idea is commitment. If you hesitate, if you don't finish, if you engage partially or don't think of yourself as already dead, then your opponent picks up on it and you get punched in the face (if you're facing fists) or sliced up (if you're facing a sword). It's another version of suggesting a jump in the lake. We need to face our fears head-on and completely.

This lesson was reinforced when I once turned to a friend as the two of us and her son were hoisted high in the air on a bungee cord over an amusement park that kept dwindling far below. "You must really like these thrill rides," I said.

"No, I hate heights, especially airplanes."

I momentarily forgot my own trepidation, wondering about this new perspective.

"I'm doing this to get over my fear," she continued. "Pull the ripcord."

The lesson here is simple but profound: True growth requires facing fear directly, without hesitation or retreat. In martial arts and in life, it's not enough to merely go through the motions. When the sword is drawn or the challenge is set before us, you can't afford to hold back. By fully committing to the moment and overcoming the restraints of fear, you can find the courage and clarity needed to succeed. It's a reminder that the most important moments often come when we're forced to step into the unknown, trusting that the only way forward is through.

 ***Commit fully, and face your challenges head-on.*** 

Thanks, Grandma!

I first came across an invaluable tool for prioritization, Grandma's Rule, as an unexpected side benefit of conflict. I'd asked a friend and colleague who'd just returned from two weeks of intensive leadership training in the mountains of Colorado what she'd learned.

"Two things," she said. "First, if you want to go far in a big company, you have to work on a big, critical, cross-organizational project. That gives you exposure."

Since she was returning to lead just such a project, we agreed she had that one covered.

"And the second?" I asked.

"You have to have had a difficult boss."

We grinned at each other like my lab partner and I did when we discovered that a clear, odorless liquid from distillation of wood was highly flammable. "Check," we said in unison.

Both my boss and I had had several years of exceptional results. He'd recently taken over his new role, and though we struggled hard at it, we couldn't seem to get along. Given a series of similar strains with other employees, my friend and I, along with the rest of the team and our boss, were all heading to a mandated, externally led, week-long off-site training to learn to work better together.

In preparation, we'd taken several tests, including the Myers–Briggs Type Indicator that measures preferred style for interacting with others. Most people I've worked with have been through this at some point in their careers. If you've ever had to measure whether you're an introvert or an extrovert, a thinker or a feeler, a judger or a perceiver, you've taken it too. Although some people have described it as "worthless psychobabble," it led to a transformative insight the first day of our session.

We lined up around a long table according to how we scored on one of the attributes, intuitive versus sensing. Oversimplifying, intuitive people tend to string a couple of facts together and jump to a pattern, while sensing people like documentation and double-checking. I was on the intuitive side of the table. People with scores near 50 percent intuitive were clustered at the end to my left, and the closer they got to 100 percent, they spread out in a half bell curve on my side. I was alone at the far end of the table, off-the-charts intuitive. As I looked across the table I saw the same pattern. A group barely falling into the sensing category gathered at the far end, others distributed along the side based on their sensing scores, and directly across from me was my polar opposite, my boss. We finally had a revelation into our challenges with each other.

After the session and a four-and-a-half-hour dinner at a local restaurant during which we aired our mutual differences, we achieved a halfway decent daily working relationship. The other step we took to improve was that we were both paired with a coach. Sometimes people hear this in a work environment and think, "Uh oh. This person's on the way out." But this coach was excellent at helping me discover some pretty deep introspection. He also gave me some useful tools, one of which was Grandma's Rule, which is simply this: Eat your vegetables before you can have dessert.

In practical execution, this means doing the hardest thing on our list first. If we instead start with what's easiest, the brain tends to rebel. Rather than a sense of relief or accomplishment when we finish, we get a sense of dread because the next thing on our list is harder. When we instead begin with what's difficult, we're rewarded when we finish because the next task is easier.

I got so accustomed to using this technique at work that my team knew how their annual performance review would go based on where they were in the lineup. No one wanted to be first, and everyone wanted to be last. I had to have my assistant start scheduling them at random.

As with most rules, there are exceptions:

- Sometimes you need to start with a smaller problem first, because you need to build up some muscle, some expertise, before tackling the big item.
- Sometimes a problem needs to be bigger before you can solve it. In an old episode of *Mr. Wizard* about the coefficient of friction, he tilted a board covered in different materials until an object

slid off, showing a certain amount of inertia needed to be overcome before an object moved. Similarly, a certain amount of organizational friction needs to be overcome before a team realizes a problem is worth fixing and rallies around solving it. The problem needs to be big enough to compete with others.

- Another exception comes from a conversation I had with the famous author Malcolm Gladwell at an industry event. Sometimes problems go away if you sleep on them and do nothing. I've gotten to the end of a busy day to find a string of phone calls, texts, or emails that I didn't manage to get to. The first one is often frantic and describes a crisis, and the most recent one tells you "Never mind. I figured it out."

Despite the occasional exception, Grandma's Rule applies most of the time. Homework due tomorrow? Do the report you don't want to do before the one that's not so bad. Working around the house? Scrub those pots and pans first before folding laundry while listening to music. Conversation coming up that you're afraid of? You know what to do.

 *Do the hard stuff first.* 

The Reserve Tank

Nassim Nicholas Taleb wrote a series of books on how systems tend to break down over time and that when they do, it's all of a sudden. His focus is on financial markets, but he also uses examples from real life, such as airplane delays and traffic gridlock in New York. It's almost always because a system gets stressed to the limit, and once a breaking point is reached it falls apart. Whether it's an extra resource or downtime, we need slack to avoid this happening.

For example, the first time my wife and I took the kids to Disney World it was fun, but a lot less than it could've been. I rousted us all early enough to get to the big rides before others and to see almost everything in all the parks, and I marched all of us around like little soldiers, trying to pack activities into every available second, until we were exhausted. One evening, after a park-closing fireworks display, my eight-year-old fell asleep on my shoulder as we returned to the parking lot. So the next time we went, we built in time. We got to the parks when we got there, stayed a few hours until we were tired, then went back and hung around the pool at our hotel. When we felt like it, we went back in the afternoons or evenings, which was much more fun. Slack helped.

Another example is when I went skiing with a friend and old boss of mine, who billed himself as the world's fastest smoking marathoner. Run after run, he'd barrel down the mountain nonstop, with me struggling to keep up. By the fifth run my legs were wobbly, so I stopped partway down to rest. I found him at the bottom, not in the chairlift line waiting for me to go up again but smoking a cigarette. "I thought you were just going to keep following me all day and I was never going to get to smoke," he said. The rest of the day I made numerous stops, and we were both a lot happier. Taking the breaks helped me enjoy skiing more.

Slack can also present itself. On a work trip to Amsterdam, I was walking the city the day before a big meeting, enjoying the many beautiful canal-lined streets. But there were also busy narrow canyons peppered with shop after shop selling cheesy T-shirts, knickknacks, knockoff pottery, and wooden shoes. The barrage of kitsch growing overwhelming, I ducked through a narrow archway, thinking it might cut across to another street. It didn't, but what a pleasant surprise I found! The tumult of the street disappeared as I entered a carefully tended flower garden within a cloister that had stone contemplation benches surrounding a central pool replenished by lightly trickling water. I'm not sure how long I sat there, but it was a nice recharge.

Even in the middle of a business trip, it's important to take time for yourself.

This is essential in personal finance, where we advise people who are saving for retirement to have several months of savings on hand in case of emergency. That might be for an unexpected car repair, being forced out of work for medical reasons, or getting laid off. A safety savings account is a form of slack.

The same concept applies at work, where I've seen a particular scenario play out several times. After much horse trading and angst, a company has carefully projected and agreed to a budget, and the available resources are allocated for projects. Somewhere around the second quarter, there's an unexpected emergency that diverts resources and budget dollars, requiring a restacking, restart, or cessation of planned projects. As a side effect, the budget is often underspent because resources aren't available to fully execute plans. This often results in pressure to spend everything before the year ends, even if it means unnecessary spending.

You have to set aside some resources, both funding and people, and leave some slack in your timelines to handle the unexpected.

I first heard the following parable while hiking in the White Mountains with my dad, friends, and three kids. When my dad insisted we stop to rest, another older hiker agreed and told this story: Two lumberjacks, an older man and a younger man, were both working in a forest, competing to see who could cut the most wood.

The younger man, stronger and full of vitality, chopped away all day without ceasing, sweat pouring from his face. Every so often he heard the older man stop, and he assumed he was getting tired. When they reached the end of the day and compared results, the older man had chopped much more than the younger one.

"You kept stopping! What were you doing? I thought you were tired."

"I was sharpening my axe."

> ***Build in slack, a break, a relief valve for the pressure, and you'll appreciate what you're doing more and have a higher likelihood of success.***

Changing the Target

I once took a year-long class with participants from various sectors including industry, nonprofit, and government. Among them were a former gang member turned preacher, a big-city treasurer, the head of the Connecticut Girl Scouts, the head of the Connecticut NAACP, and a local school superintendent.

One of our earliest activities was an Outward Bound course, which involved outdoor challenges. On the first day, we canoed down a river from New Hampshire to Maine, with the option of paddling eight, ten, or twelve miles. Wanting to be the "best," everyone chose the longest distance. When we finished and the guide asked, "How do you feel?" I was surprised that some of us were exhausted and regretted choosing the longer route.

The following day, we split into teams for an orienteering challenge, using compasses and topographical maps to find and record hidden locations in the woods. We again had the option of setting our own goal "however you want; find one or twenty." Trying to learn from the prior day's lesson, we set a modest target of seven locations, but we supplemented our aim with a secondary objective: making sure that by the end of the exercise, everyone on the team would know how to use a compass and read a map, and would have had a chance to lead the group. We found nine locations, encouraged everyone to take a turn leading, and returned to camp smiling and laughing.

Meanwhile, one team had set a target of fourteen, and despite finding twelve locations argued and complained throughout the search, continuing right into dinner. I heard one member saying, "I didn't know what the experts were doing, but I never got a chance to learn because we were so intent on winning."

This contrast between our team's experience and theirs highlighted the important lesson that setting realistic goals and prioritizing teamwork leads to better outcomes.

> *Set your objectives appropriately, to balance a stretch with learning, and to focus on what's most important.*

Time for Tea

Mindful reflection has a similar benefit.

As our kids got older, my wife and I started using a trick to help them appreciate a trip we were on. On the last day, because we'd taken the advice to leave slack in our day, we were sitting around relaxing instead of hurrying off to catch the last bit of something, and we reviewed the best and worst parts of the trip, with a focus on the best. It's a way of ingraining the details into your mind, whether of major travel or a visit to a park.

The technique of reviewing can work with even a brief moment that made your day. Pause, and go through what each of your five senses is experiencing. For example, after the first half of a long bike ride, I stopped for a snack at a reservoir. It had been overcast all day, but the sun was poking through the clouds, and a golden ray of light was shining on the reservoir surface (sight). An eagle flew out of a nearby tree and right through the light beam, then landed with a rustle in a tree nearby (sound). I was crunching on a granola bar (sound and taste) and enjoying cold water after a tough ride (also taste) as the wind dried the sweat on my legs (touch) and the pines gave off a balsam scent (smell). It's no wonder authors are advised to describe a scene with multiple senses and not just visual cues.

In a similar situation, when our son was about four, he accompanied me to the bottom of the driveway to put the trash out. I started back up to the house and then realized he wasn't with me. I turned to find him staring up at the sky. "Look at all the stars, Dad."

I had taken the trash out as a chore several hundred times by then. This was the first time I just stopped and stared at the universe as if I'd never seen it before.

Nobody, nothing, is perfect. Stop waiting for that perfect day. Do it now. Put down your phone or stop watching TV. Appreciate the person you're with if you're with someone, anything besides entertaining yourself with someone else's work effort.

 *Pausing to reflect can provide both new insights and appreciation.* 

You Again

Grandma's Rule can become so ingrained that it's hard to think in any other direction. I still feel guilty (but only for a second) when I skip the meal and go straight to dessert because that's what I like.

There's a lot of support for the approach of working hard and "earning" something before you have the "right" to enjoy it. Aesop told the parable of the grasshopper and the ant a long time before modern business schools recommended prioritization matrices or Benjamin Spock provided child-rearing guidance. Yet sometimes this ordered, serial approach isn't best.

Psychologist Abraham Maslow first published his well-known hierarchy of needs in 1943. Most people have come to believe that the hierarchy needs to be fulfilled in order, that we progress from the basic physiological requirements of food, water, and sleep, and only then to safety and security, then to love and belonging, then to self-esteem, and finally to self-actualization. More modern interpretations, especially in a motivational context, describe the value of working on a slice of each of these layers all at the same time. It's good to do a little for yourself while you're ticking the basics off the list, such as enjoying a movie instead of working until 10:00 every night or volunteering somewhere even when you don't have a lot of free time.

This approach of keeping a little for yourself shows up in other fields as well. In retirement planning, for example, yes you should set aside money early and often for that future someday, but at the same time it's a good idea to splurge occasionally. Clark Howard, a long-time radio and television commentator on saving, spending wisely, and avoiding fraud, has often given similar advice to someone who has just come into a surprise source of funds, such as an inheritance from Grandma. He suggests they take a small portion and spend it on themselves, or they'll be tempted to go after the whole bucket of money they've set aside for later.

Similarly, whether from a career or personal development standpoint, it's certainly a good idea to spend a lot of time early on mastering the basics of a skill. But it's also very helpful to spend time doing things that aren't task-specific, such as meeting a lot of people, being curious and asking questions, finding out about strategic direction, and understanding how the different parts of a business fit together.

One additional consideration when it comes to how to spend your time is how to best replenish your energy. If you're classified as an introvert on that Myers–Briggs test, you might best recharge with dedicated downtime, while an extrovert might do just the opposite and seek out a party. Both are okay depending on what you need. Likewise, if creativity gives you some juice, then get yourself a hobby as an adult. And don't feel guilty about pursuing it. You need it to be your best.

> ***Take care of yourself.***

Summary

The way you approach your work (and life) can be just as important as the work itself. Keep these lessons in mind:

- ***Be confident. Be aware. Make it about the other person. Anticipate.***

- *When faced with a new experience or a challenge, throw yourself into it.*
- *Commit fully and face your challenges head-on.*
- *Remember Grandma's Rule: Do the hard and uncomfortable stuff first.*
- *Keep some slack in your life and work.*
- *Set appropriate objectives that bring out your best.*
- *Pause to reflect, appreciate, and be present.*
- *Invest in yourself, constantly look for opportunities to improve, and recharge when necessary.*

Chapter 4

The Importance
of Relationships and Culture

Relationships with others are foundational to continued growth, and they extend in every direction. We have relationships with teammates, employees, supervisors, senior leaders, industry influencers, customers, and even competitors. There are some useful rules of thumb for building, maintaining, and getting the most out of relationships, including the benefits of creating bonding experiences, making our interactions personal and relevant to others, and maintaining integrity.

In this chapter, we'll cover the following questions that arise in building and maintaining relationships:

- *How can relationships help me with problems? With learning and growing?*
- *What are some ways to engage those I'm building a relationship with?*
- *What should I say, and when should I say it?*
- *How do I align my interests with those of others?*
- *When should I rely on a relationship?*
- *How do ethics play into relationships?*

I'm Here to Help

Working with retirement plans for cities, states, and counties around the US presented a wide variety of experiences, some funny, some infuriating, and some unexpected. The variations from one governmental client to another are as pronounced as the differences between one part of the country and another: jambalaya versus chowder, eggs and grits versus huevos rancheros, chicken-fried steak versus avocado toast. The people are different, the cultures are different, and the priorities are different. There is one common element, though: In any market, relationships are critical.

Governmental employees, at all levels, tend to be "people people," so working with governmental entities was a natural hothouse for learning about relationships. There are a few things you need to know about marketing to and maintaining a relationship with a governmental entity, starting with the similarities they all share despite their many differences in size, constitution, local culture, and politics:

- There's always a small community of connected individuals who can provide you with an introduction and some influence so that your story at least gets heard. Unlike the government we expect when renewing our license or registration with the DMV, you can almost always find dedicated public servants who could be making three or four times as much in the private sector. There's always pride in the city, state, county, or region represented as well as in the people who live and work there.

- Decision-making is distributed and made by committee. If you visit a small- or mid-sized company, you can get a decision from a single conversation with the president or treasurer. If you work with a government entity using an identical set of facts, you need to provide the political person with some positive press, the treasurer with some cost savings, the head of the police or fire union with a story of better benefits for their constituents, and the administrative person with a significant enough reduction in their work that you make their job easier, but not so much that they lose it. The approach to each individual needs to be tailored to them.

- Many governmental employees live in a constant state of concern about their jobs. If there's a turnover in administration at election time, priorities and personnel may shift dramatically. They can be hyperfocused on budgets, and they're big into process and proof. All this results in an organizational or collective reluctance to change.

Each of these factors affects governmental relationships, and while no two clients are alike, one constant remains: the need for patience, flexibility, and a keen understanding of the decision-making processes that govern public sector work.

I knew none of that, however, when I took on responsibility for this market.

Additionally, the new head of retirement, a blustery knock-down, drag-out screamer from Salomon Brothers on Wall Street who once ripped a corded telephone out of the wall and threw it at someone over an answer he didn't like, had just initiated the third consultant review of the government business. He'd undertaken these reviews expecting a recommendation to exit, and when each of the first two recommended staying in, he fired them in turn and hired another. Our company's reputation, despite several years in the business, had dimmed from prior years too. The first piece of external mail I found on my desk the day I started was a returned bid with a handwritten note: "If we wanted your bid, we would have asked for it."

I needed to get to know this market quickly, before the third consultant's report came back. So, I promptly made two mistakes, and both were based on a misunderstanding of mindset and relationships.

Tractors and Race Cars

Our most long-standing customer was a Midwestern state, and the two salesmen who'd brought it in during the early seventies had not only built terrific relationships but written the legislation that first allowed governmental organizations to offer a 457 plan, the governmental cousin of a 401(k). In my initial conversation with them, when I was trying to gather as many perspectives on the market as I could, I inadvertently came across as questioning their credibility and was hung up on. I flew out to mend fences, met them in a small local restaurant, watched my hand disappear into an iron grip when we shook, and sat down to eat. Both men owned farms, and although they wore suits, they'd just stripped off the overalls they had on over them while selling a John Deere Gator. Taking the time to apologize in person (and finishing the side of beef that overflowed my plate), set us on the right track. We parted in much better shape, and over the years they became good friends and sources of valuable advice.

Another early mistake was a bid on a Southeastern state. We had a terrific long-term relationship but were in a race with several other companies to maintain our position. In my naivete and hubris, and overriding the recommendation of a team member, I got too casual with the wording in our bid and failed to meet a technical requirement. After a call from an irate relationship manager a few weeks later telling us we'd been kicked out, I flew south to get back in.

One of those people of influence I described earlier, a top lobbyist for NASCAR, described what was going to happen in our meeting with the state: "You're going to walk in and apologize for the confusing wording that was subject to such unclear interpretation. Then the chair is going to yell at you for a few minutes. You're going to sit there and take it and then everything will be okay and you'll be back in."

That's exactly what happened, and the departures afterward were so cordial that you never would've known there was any yelling. It was all for show.

> *It's easy to destroy a relationship, and you can sometimes use an existing one to repair the damage.*

It's a Team Thing

Through the course of the next fourteen years, we obtained approval to stay in the governmental business, wrote several new plans, and returned the business to profitability. By the time I left, we'd moved from seventh in market position to fourth and grown from eleven US states as clients to twenty-six, one relationship at a time.

It was hard work. Putting your best foot forward for a governmental deal is exhausting. Besides meeting exact requirements and chasing down the FedEx guy, there's the ordeal of a final presentation. You bid, and once the field has narrowed to three or four finalists you present in person as a team. A representative example is a bid on our largest West Coast city's plan. Our team of ten rehearsed the night before and retired to bed about 2 a.m., too tired to do anything other than stumble over our words. The next morning we presented, and we got one of only two ovations ever from a finals committee, after which we high-fived in the parking lot. We got the deal, and it was one of the best feelings in the world to work together with others toward a common goal.

To reproduce that feeling for others, we put together a program for about two hundred leaders based on an imaginary client, the City of San Pretendo. It was replete with a documentary-style video of the preparations the night before and a live mock-committee presentation in which I played the part of our company president, who threatened me with "I'm going to get you" as his entire senior team practically rolled on the floor with laughter at the spot-on imitation.

 *Struggling through a challenge with others forges long-lasting bonds and a sense of camaraderie.* 

Live, Local, and Late-Breaking

One of the most important elements of communication with any governmental plan, especially given their diverse audiences and objectives, is keeping your message relevant and personal.

When we presented to a committee, we'd work to tailor the presentation to them and tap into some of their local pride. In one southern coastal state, for example, we were quoted a vendor price of over $30,000 to record a sample enrollment video for state employees. We instead shot the footage locally for $1,200, got a locally known newscaster to do the voice-over for free, then put images on the screen of all the committee members' favorite places, including the golf course on which one had scored a hole-in-one, the college one taught at, and the horse country where one liked to visit. Home run.

In a southern city known for its music, we did something similar when we presented a map of the city with pushpins representing each of the governmental facilities—blue for police, red for fire, and green for municipal. They loved seeing themselves represented. And in New Hampshire, we talked about being able to cover the state from Coös to Concord, and the selection panel cited our pronunciation of the former (Co-ahss) as a sign of our familiarity, a factor that led to us being awarded the relationship.

In Massachusetts, however, we made a near fatal mistake. Our guy in charge of employee interactions couldn't pronounce any of the place names (Peabody, Billerica, Quincy, and especially Worcester, the latter you should look up online for a laugh), so we substituted in someone else. As a corollary, I almost lost a deal in Memphis when referencing the Peabody Hotel there. I caught myself just in time and pronounced it the standard way rather than the Massachusetts way.

A challenge to personalization is that your own team is composed of different people, which can lead to inconsistency when you're carrying multiple messages. For a presentation to a northern Rust Belt city, for instance, we had to answer a question about a pending lawsuit, which we'd heard our chief competitor had planted with a committee member who wanted to retain them instead of replacing them with us. We prepared our head of marketing, who had a penchant for talking too long, on what to say: "Lawsuits? Yes, we occasionally will get a lawsuit, as any company does. This one has no merit and will not impact our ability to administer your plan." Instead when the potentially damaging question came up, he answered somewhat differently: "Oh, lawsuits! You want to talk lawsuits? You wouldn't believe how many we have!" He then went on at length until one of our team members interrupted to ask whether it would have any impact on our ability to administer the plan. He got back on script and sat down.

> *Tailor your message to your audience for the greatest positive impact on the relationship, and be sure to maintain consistency.*

Not on the Map

When through a complex bid process our team won what was then the largest new contract we'd ever bid on for a West Coast city, we traveled to meet them and their consultant in person. During our first meeting with them, both the city and their consultant admitted not really knowing what they were doing, not having switched providers in seventeen years. We were straightforward and acknowledged that we hadn't done a deal this large before either but would make sure it went right. It was a risk to be so clear, but it paid off.

"Thank you for your comportment."

We developed a solid relationship, and I landed on a piece of advice I've given to countless folks about how to handle a difficult situation.

> *When in doubt, tell the truth.*

A Big Number

Another memorable governmental trip was when I flew to a southern gulf state for lunch. While this may sound extravagant, they had grown from a small plan to over $1 billion in assets, and we wanted to celebrate with them. They maintained their down-home and cost-conscious approach, even though we paid for lunch, by opting for a small second-floor restaurant bedecked with red-and-white checkered tablecloths, paper plates, and plastic forks.

It was a challenge to describe how big a billion was. I first channeled A. Whitney Brown, a commentator on *Saturday Night Live* in the mid-1980s who when China's population reached a billion joked about that meaning that even if you're one in a million, there are a thousand people just like you. That got a chuckle, but what really helped them appreciate how much their team had accomplished was a metaphor closer to home. I reflected that from far away the Mississippi River is still big but it's hard to detect its strength and motion. Up close, however, it's immense and powerful. It was like that with the state's retirement plan. From a distance, a billion was just another number, but up close, doing the work the team did with one individual after another, it was possible to see the powerful effect of making sure people have enough money to retire on. Working together, we were making a difference.

In similar fashion, when my wife sold several dozen winter coats to Mainers in a single weekend and I asked her how she'd done it, she first emphasized that she didn't put anyone in clothing that didn't make them look better than when they walked in. After I pushed some more when I found out that in addition to top sales she had the lowest returns in the store, she talked about reinforcement: "I remind them how good they look when they walk out the door. They're happy with what they bought and don't bring it back."

> *Celebrate successes and progress*
> *with your customers.*

Watch What You Ask For

Another challenging bid was for a large Northern California city with multiple providers. We managed $100 million in assets, our competitor $350 million. They'd spent two years convincing the city to consolidate all assets with a single provider for efficiency, so when we were called to a public hearing for bid discussion, the odds of us keeping our piece were low.

Whether because of the highly dangerous nature of their jobs or their communal nature, police officers and firefighters have some of the highest participation rates in and knowledge of their voluntary retirement plans. Though they may have each other's backs every day on the job, in a relationship akin to that of siblings they compete fiercely over their preferences for retirement plan providers and provisions.

On the morning of the hearing, we leveraged a relationship by meeting with a firefighter familiar with the committee discussions to gather some intel and a few pointers. We discovered that the two sides of the day's argument were well-established; the fire union would support us staying in, and the police union would encourage consolidation.

The hearing itself, however, was a mobbed hubbub of conversation so loud we could barely hear each other as I looked around to guess who was who and on which side. After an orchestrated parade of individual city employees standing up to sing our competitor's praises, as well as an intermittent grilling during which I answered sporadic questions from the panel, one of the committee members argued the benefits of consolidation, which instigated a lot of positive head-nodding. Our fire union committee member, without a change in tone or emphasis, moved to consolidate, but he added a surprise. He suggested the city move all the assets to us.

Before there was an opportunity for audience opposition, the motion was seconded. The chair had asked for committee discussion, but having none he called for a vote. In a matter of seconds, we not only kept our smaller position but took over the entire plan.

Stunned, the spokesperson for our competitor rose to protest but was told the vote had already been made. He turned bright red and let off a tirade, but the committee members casually got up and walked out.

 **_Leverage your favorable relationships._** 

The General, the Money Man, and the Presidential Candidate

Sometimes, personalizing your message can work in tandem with leveraging relationships.

I've already mentioned a southern state in which an early mistake required relationship-mending through a NASCAR lobbyist. We returned to that state a few years later when they introduced a new retirement plan, for which we estimated potential assets of over $1 billion.

To close the deal, two colleagues and I surmounted travel challenges by flying partway to our destination and driving the remaining six hours, skirting a midnight traffic jam by maneuvering a decrepit Crown Vic through a deserted railroad yard, only to arrive at 2 a.m. to find out from our regional salesman that we were going to get booted from the arrangement. Not taking no for an answer, we strategized how to use relationships to overturn what seemed to be a decision already made and how to get back in.

The first step was to present to a lower-level committee the next day, and the second step, if we survived the first, was to argue our case to an approval committee composed of the state treasurer, a retired army general, and the then-sitting US president's brother (later a candidate for the office himself). After a short sleep, we encountered an unexpected obstacle during my opening remarks to the lower-level committee when the head of a teachers' group corrected my use of the word "enormity" to describe the magnitude of our potential responsibility: "That's not what that means, you know. Enormity doesn't have anything to do with size. It means great wickedness."

This felt like I was reliving the same situation that the NASCAR lobbyist got me out of years earlier, only now I was in front of a live audience. Thinking my vocabulary was good but not wanting to signal the apparent impertinence that an argument might imply, I scrambled for an answer: "Thank you. My parents are both teachers, as are many of my relatives. I have great respect for teaching. I appreciate the correction. What would you suggest I use instead?"

She landed on "enormousness," but ever since I've just used "size." She was the first of her colleagues to advance us to the next round.

I looked it up when I got home, and she was right. I forgot about it other than as a lesson in showing respect, until President Obama's acceptance speech when he talked about the "enormity" of the job he was coming into. I yelled at the screen about what it really meant, but I don't think he heard me.

We expected the subsequent approval hearing to be highly charged, similar to the one on the West Coast, so we tailored our advance communications to the audience. The meeting with the reputedly tightfisted treasurer was in a garage. Our salesperson, a veteran of the Iraq War, met with the army general, and one of my colleagues with White House experience met with the president's brother. The personalization, combined with another factor, helped us to stand out from the eight companies vying for the four available spots. While each of their nearly identical White male representatives presented nearly identical arguments for inclusion, and though they were backed by carefully curated public testimonials, our speakers were a short, stocky army vet with a shaved head, and a tall, elegant, African American woman.

The committee was stone-faced throughout, but by the time our turn came up they had approved the four we predicted and rejected the remainder.

The general and treasurer asked tough questions of our two speakers and still didn't change their expressions. However, when it came time to vote, they described our presentation as the best of the day and readmitted our bid on an exception.

When a rejected competitor asked to be readmitted on the same grounds, the president's brother asked our army vet whether he thought we should let them in.

Standing at attention, he simply replied, "No, sir. I do not."

"So, we've just made an exception for you, and you don't think we should extend it to anyone else? That's pretty brassy," (he used a somewhat more colorful term).

"That's right, sir."

The stoic general laughed and exchanged glances with the president's brother, who closed the meeting without further comment. Although in the end the arrangement accumulated only about 2 percent of the original $1 billion estimate, we got back in.

> *Personalized communication is even more*
> *powerful when combined with relationships.*
> *Both help you stand out from the pack*
> *in a positive, memorable light.*

Wicked Big Deal

The largest plan we ever bid on was for the Commonwealth of Massachusetts (as with Virginia, Kentucky, and Pennsylvania, you don't say "State"). It was $3.5 billion in assets but had some complex structural issues.

I had no good way to price anything that large, so I triangulated an answer from multiple perspectives, an approach I often espouse with pricing teams because the multiple viewpoints have more value than going deep with only a single perspective. It was useful when we met with the CEO of retirement, who at one point argued for a fee of about half the price I'd projected because there was an acquisition pending and he wanted to make the deal. We settled in the middle, later finding from Freedom of Information filings that the multi-perspective estimate was accurate.

After another multistep struggle that one of my colleagues often described as "survive and advance," similar to the annual NCAA basketball tournament and including some on-the-fly pricing changes for large amounts, we arrived in the evening before the final announcement of a winner and received the following intelligence: "It's down to you and the incumbent company. Yours is a compelling bid, but I'm just not sure there's enough here to warrant a move. Can you put together a story as to why we should do this?"

Not only did we do that, but I drafted a press release they could use to award the business to us. That was more than argumentation for them; it made the decision easy. The next day when the actual release ran awarding us the business, it contained verbatim what we'd sent them.

 *You can help a relationship by providing someone with what they need most.* 

Shine On

This process of listening to what others need, and from that helping them look good, can help decisions and transactions move forward. It's not just about presenting a good argument. Building relationships helps.

For example, we had won one of the retirement plans in a mid-Atlantic city, but we needed regulatory approval before we could take it over, and the state's insurance commissioner was dragging his feet approving. After hearing him frustrated over what to say at an upcoming speaking engagement, I sent him some talking points for his speech. The day after he spoke and was warmly applauded, we were approved.

In the same city, once approved, our first task was to fire the current investment manager, who was the nephew of the disgraced former mayor. The client, wary of his connections, left the "dirty work" to us. Taking this burden from them helped cement our relationship.

In another example, a friend and colleague left the firm to work for a consultant, and his request for help pulled me away from a team outing. "I need you on a call in ten minutes to ask you some questions about your bid," he said. "I don't know anything about stable value [a topic I'd worked with and been published on since 1982], and I need a few questions I can ask you."

Ten minutes later, he was introduced by his boss as the firm's expert and asked me the same questions I'd just fed him. We won.

> **Give people what they need to shine, and you'll be invaluable to them.**

Unexpected Lessons

Sometimes how you ask a question sets the tone for a relationship, even a new one. I learned this twice and at, of all places, airline counters.

The first was on a work trip to Hawaii, but with a full day in a conference room with Subway catering, a challenging presentation, and a quick turnaround, it was less glamorous than you might imagine. The learning experience was the result of running through the Atlanta airport and missing a connecting flight by two minutes. At the rescheduling counter, I waited in a long line, tried the phone, and after spending an hour on hold was directed by the operator to the same desk in Atlanta near where I was standing. I circled back to the queue, watching disappointed passengers leave one by one.

Here's where luck and a lesson from Robert Cialdini's *Influence*, a book I'd been reading on the first leg of the trip, came in handy. Cialdini explains that providing any reason (even a vague one) makes people more likely to say yes. He provides the example of testers interrupting people who are about to use a copy machine. The tester asks whether it would be okay if they made their copies first, explaining they have an important presentation for their boss. Almost everyone allowed the interrupter in. When testers interrupted in the next phase, they left out any reason for their need. Some got in, but many were told to wait their turn. A third group of testers was more open-ended with their interruption, asking if it would be okay to make their copies first simply because they needed to make some copies. The positive response rate was almost as high as the first group, which suggests that it doesn't matter what your reason is, you just have to provide one.

So, when I got to the counter, I provided a reason for my request: "Could you possibly rebook me to fly to Hawaii today instead of tomorrow because I have a really important presentation to give that affects about ten thousand people who work there?"

That was the first piece of luck. The second was that the guy in front of me had been abusive to the agent. I arrived not just with a specific request but with a bright, calming smile by contrast. She went out of her way to get me booked on another airline so I could get there on time.

This lesson came up again during a trip back from New Orleans with our head of sales, the one who'd once worked for a US president and who proudly displayed his top-secret clearance to try for an upgrade. The agent politely declined, saying, "I'm sorry sir, but there doesn't appear to be anything available."

I, however, had left my wallet on the counter, revealing a photo of my kids as the agent and I chatted. The agent asked about them, and I shared the story of adopting them from Chile. Without me asking, she upgraded my seat and handed me another ticket. "Take this to your friend," she said. "Let him know you got him upgraded too."

> ***Ask nicely, and with a reason, to quickly
> break the ice and build rapport.***

New Mates

Working with governmental entities wasn't the only place I learned unexpected lessons about relationships and culture. One was through my passion for chess.

In Amsterdam, I visited a local plaza named after the only Dutch World Chess champion, where I arrived to discover two people competing on a life-sized chess set surrounded by a crowd of cheering spectators. I really wanted to participate, but there was a long line intersplicing what felt like a contentiously territorial prison yard. I found two elderly gentlemen sitting nearby playing speed chess. Despite me not knowing Dutch and them not knowing English besides "Hello," I was able to pantomime my way into playing a few games with them. It was one of the most fun experiences I've had while traveling.

I've used that interest in chess to meet the two-time holder of the Guinness-certified world record for playing the most people at once in a simultaneous exhibition, as well as a group of players I stumbled across in a Manhattan mall.

Similarly, if you meet someone from Europe, Africa, or South America, you can almost always quickly generate a conversation about football (soccer to Americans).

> ***You can leverage common interests
> to build a quick connection.***

Hans Brinker and the Silver-Haired Union Negotiator

Even casual conversations can be beneficial if you remain aware of your environment.

On that same trip to Amsterdam, stirred awake from a jet-lag-induced inadvertent nap in a dimly lit auditorium featuring a droning speaker, I struck up a conversation at a stand-up lunch with a woman who looked to be in her mid-seventies. Normally at an event you've traveled to, it's a good idea to work your way around the room and meet everyone, but her stories of the Dutch retirement mindset and practices and of union and political conflicts were too fascinating to move on to anyone else. She seemed to know every minute detail, and she injected life and color into her descriptions of the political wrangling that smacked of my work in the US governmental markets.

Returning to the auditorium, I was determined not to fall asleep again. There was no need to worry. The woman I'd chatted with at lunch was introduced as the next speaker. She was the former Dutch equivalent of our Secretary of Labor and had made her mark by being a tough negotiator with the unions.

 *Stay curious in any conversation, and don't underestimate the person you're speaking with.* 

Step Away from the Vehicle

I'd like to return stateside for another lesson about relationships.

Just as with an insurance commissioner stymied by a speech or a new consultant wanting to demonstrate expertise, looking good is likely an objective for all of us. There are times, though, when behavior goes beyond a desire to look good and people involved with a potential sale go too far. Those are times when we need to terminate a relationship. There are three deals I walked away from, and I'm glad I did.

The first was straightforward. We were doing well on a bid for a very large Midwestern city when a "consultant" the city had hired demanded an exorbitant commission, and it just didn't feel right. I checked with our ethics attorney, who'd provided an unbiased investigation into a disgraced governor and cleaned up a college basketball recruiting program after a scandal. She checked with her counterpart in the city, who told us to "stay away from that guy." We did.

Another large Midwestern city, known for its manufacturing, was more of a mess when we vied to take over business from the incumbent. First the city made a huge mistake by establishing a decision-making committee with an even number of voting members. After several tied votes, meaning no change, one of the committee members allegedly agreed to provide a parking space closer to the building if another member would change their vote, tipping the decision in our favor. But when some members were on vacation, a reconvened committee reversed the vote. I've since learned that unless you have a near unanimous decision, you're better off not taking the deal, but I didn't know that at the time, so we worked undeterred to regain support.

I met individually with key committee members, guided by a close colleague. Though they each seemed above board and of high integrity themselves, the atmosphere surrounding them was not. In one memorable meeting, a heavily bejeweled man in the next booth entertained a request to "help out with that cement contract out at the airport."

Though the effort to connect seemed worthwhile when the committee later voted us back in, the same reversal happened again a few weeks later, and we were once more voted out.

While debating whether to visit committee members yet again, we got word that a large technology company had walked away from a city contract worth several hundred million dollars because of the same antics we were seeing. We decided to let it go and cut our losses. Once again, the decision proved right, as a few years later at least one of the characters involved in the city's constant vote-changing was indicted.

The top prize for bad behavior, I think, has to go to a state in the Deep South. After our successful finals presentation to a twenty-eight-person union panel instead of a usual small committee, the state's reps came to Hartford for a due diligence trip, and we spotted several red flags. One of note was when we hosted the delegation at a very nice local restaurant. Near the end of the meal, I heard yelling in the hallway outside the room we were in. It went on for a while but eventually died down. I later found out that some of the delegates were pocketing silverware, sugar containers, and even some crystal, and our head of sales had offered compensation to the maître d'.

What completely broke an already uncomfortable deal was a dispute over a different type of compensation. It's common in governmental bids that the winning provider reimburses the city, state, or county for legitimate education about worker benefits. It has to be disclosed in advance in bid documents, and the reimbursement process requires strict documentation. This state wanted a reimbursement many times over the typical level, wanted it to go to a general fund, and didn't want to provide documentation. We didn't walk away. We ran.

Working with a subsequent employer, I learned through someone familiar with the situation that the winning provider, who'd met the state's demands, settled a lawsuit over the terms for close to $20 million.

> ***Trust your instincts and ethics. Walking away from a bad relationship often saves you from even bigger problems down the road.***

Judgment Day

I once agreed to teach chess to my fourth-grade son and some of his elementary school classmates at our local library and community center. One Saturday, two new kids came to play, and one of the parents pulled me aside. "Watch out for those two," he whispered. "They're trouble. They're going to end up in juvie."

He'd already made an assessment of two nine-year-old kids.

The kids defied his assessment, were engaged learners, and picked up the game rapidly. Their mothers dropped in several weeks later to tell me that they'd both brought their grades up from Ds to Bs. That felt good, and I thought nothing more of it until about a dozen years later.

Out at a local restaurant for a Mother's Day brunch, both my wife and daughter ordered a lobster frittata. When we got the meals, I thought the restaurant was sure to go out of business. There had to have been about eighty dollars' worth of lobster in each serving, for which we were charged only about twenty dollars, and we packed up two large doggie bags to go. When our server returned to the table with my card after I paid the check, she asked if we could wait a minute because the chef wanted a word with us. Out walked one of the kids who'd been predicted to land in jail.

He greeted me warmly, pronounced my last name correctly, and asked after my family. I asked him in turn whether he was still playing any chess.

"I'd like to," he responded, "but I can't."

I wasn't surprised, but a little disappointed, until he continued.

"I'm too busy. I graduate from Johnson and Wales next week, and I'm opening my own restaurant."

> **Don't judge the other party in a relationship too quickly.**

Summary

Relationships with everyone we work with and rely on are fundamental to us as human beings and are foundational to being an effective leader. Keep the following in mind as you build, maintain, and enhance your relationships while you grow:

- *Stay aware in new relationships, and remember that you don't know everything. It's easy to get off on the wrong foot. Repair damage immediately.*
- *Facing a challenge together can be a positive bonding experience.*

- *Keep it personal, relevant, and genuine. Tailor a consistent message to your audience for maximum impact and to stand out in a positive light.*
- *When in doubt, tell the truth.*
- *Celebrating success with customers, teammates, or others enhances appreciation for a relationship.*
- *You can leverage a relationship when needed, including to repair a problem.*
- *Keep in mind what benefits all parties in a relationship. You can help a relationship and prove yourself invaluable by providing someone with what they need most.*
- *Ways to build a new relationship include leveraging an area of mutual interest and asking nicely, with a reason.*
- *Stay curious in any conversation, and don't underestimate the person you're speaking with.*
- *If your ethics or your gut tells you to walk away, do it. Walking away from a bad relationship, even if it means forfeiting short-term gains, not only maintains your integrity but pays long-term dividends.*
- *Don't judge a potential relationship too quickly.*

Chapter 5

Managing the Career You Want

Looking at a career holistically, we can manage the one we want. We may not be able to control every aspect of it, but we can ensure that we're continually moving in the right direction.

In this chapter, we'll cover the following questions:

- *What plan and preparation should I have for my next step?*
- *What are my priorities in a new role?*
- *Is there a way to be noticed?*
- *How flexible should I be in establishing plans for myself?*
- *How do I manage others' perceptions of me to have the reputation I want?*
- *How do I deal with job loss?*
- *What boundaries should I set?*

Searching for That First or Next Job

Just as with searching for that first job, when you're looking for a new and better one or have had the unfortunate experience of being laid off and need to find one, cast a wide net. You may have an idea

---

77

of what you're interested in, but if you limit your scope, you miss out on a lot.

A professional job placement expert once advised following up on every offer of assistance and on every introduction to someone who might be able to help in your search. It's a form of repayment for the time someone took to provide you with the referral. It might also send you in a direction or provide an opportunity you didn't expect. With each of my searches, I developed and followed up on over two hundred contacts, including several on-site visits. Even when it wasn't a fit, it confirmed what I *didn't* want, which indirectly led me to what I did want.

As with any relationship, be nice, no matter who you're talking with and whether by phone or in person. My assistant once told me of a senior executive who always asked the opinion of the person who'd escorted a candidate into the building and would bounce anyone who treated her poorly. Build rapport with assistants and schedulers. They control everything. Take the time to get to know them, and acknowledge that you're impinging on their time as well as their boss's.

You can also use interviews to hone your story. Even if you don't get the job, you learn what others find attractive or unattractive about you. Many people go into an interview either with the concept of having to get across the information on their résumé and background or with two or three anecdotes about overcoming challenges. That preparation is valuable, but it isn't enough.

Here's the key: Wait for or instigate the right time for this message instead. Emphasizing your strengths unasked is all about you, from *your* perspective. What's much stronger is making the interview about the other person. Ask them what their biggest problems are that they're trying to solve, what their biggest challenges are, and what their ideal employee is and why. Then answer how you might help *them* solve that problem, fix *their* challenge, or create the employee *they* need. It's the same information that's on your résumé but with an entirely different positioning. By making it about them instead of you, they're eager to learn more about you.

Close the interview asking what the next steps are. Our daughter extracted the following response from an interviewer with that question: "Well, I was going to talk things over with the rest of my team, but since you asked I'm going to make you an offer right here."

Follow up on new opportunities, be appreciative of everyone you meet, and approach conversations from the other person's perspective.

A New Start

Okay, so you've landed that job or just gotten a promotion. Where do you direct your attention? How do you spend your time?

In the first several months, start by asking lots of questions. Immerse yourself in the business and learn as much as you can. Certainly, if you heard about a problem during the interview and implied your ability to help fix it, you ought to find out more about it and keep your promise. Get to work on it.

Another technique to stand out is to ask for the job that nobody else wants. It often worked for my daughter who, in her work with autistic clients, asked for the most difficult ones. Volunteering in general can also pay huge dividends. You're at low risk early in a career, so look for problems. I'll talk more about this in chapter 8.

In the same vein, if you can create a positive surprise early on, it will be remembered. This can be as simple as providing a response earlier than what was previously normal and thus expected, or it can be listening to someone who doesn't get listened to very often. Whenever I came into a new job, I preferred one with a history of problems to one where everything was running smoothly. If there's an issue, you've got something to fix. If things are running well, you can only mess it up.

 **_Take active steps early in a new role,_**
both to commit to it and to shine. 

Taking Stock

Often as we contemplate switching jobs, we're thinking beyond the immediate change. *What's my next step, then the one beyond that? What's my career path?* And we think about these things not just at the outset of a career or when we're moving between jobs, but frequently, especially at key moments, such as at the completion of a project or after an especially good or bad review.

I used to simply think that if you work hard and do the right thing, you'll rise in an organization and be rewarded for it. While that's certainly a better approach than being lazy and doing the wrong thing, deliberate intent can be helpful. You don't need an exact step-by-step set of directions, but, just as with selecting a career in the first place, knowing what you're good at and what you like as well as what you might need to work on and what you dislike is an asset.

Moving from Maine to Connecticut, I inventoried both work and personal preferences. I identified newly learned skiing as enjoyable, even though as a beginner I wasn't very good at it. When comparing it to what was motivating at work, I had an insight into the parallelism with skiing: I liked to make quick decisions with large results at stake. So when I moved, I sought out an environment with that characteristic.

Useful feedback is essential in this area, so ask for it. I say "useful" because feedback such as "You're doing a good job" is not helpful (more on this in chapter 10). You need specifics as to what went well and what didn't, as close to the event that caused that feedback as possible and from someone you trust. If you don't get it the first time, ask again.

Here's a warning on feedback: Many people seek out and listen only to the negatives. While that's fine when wanting to improve a weakness, we don't spend enough time or effort on the positives.

Upon completing a 360-degree review with input from leaders, peers, and employees, I was advised by a coach to spend about 70 percent of my time on the positives in my review, which I'd been ignoring entirely. When confronted with and obsessing over feedback that I was too quiet in meetings, she directed me to the comments telling me that when I said something, people believed I'd thought it through carefully and counted on it being true. "Speak up more often," she said, "knowing that when you say something, people believe it. Use the positive to offset the negative."

When I did exactly that, the impact was far more than being viewed as less quiet. Others listened to me more, wanted my opinion, and used my input for decisions.

Let's take the strengths and weaknesses discussion one step further. If you have a weakness that's a career-killer, such as tending to yell and scream at your employees or constantly making mistakes, then fix that. Otherwise, spend most of your time developing your strengths. As you do, look for strengths that help you stand out. By that, I mean those that play against type.

When I spoke with new actuarial students who joined the firm, and this was with multiple firms, the conversations would often go like this:

"How many of you were at or near the top of your class in math?"

Almost everyone acknowledged this.

"How many got that near perfect or perfect math SAT score?"

Again, almost everyone's hand shot up.

Now they were looking around at each other, seeing that they didn't stand out as that different, so when I advised them to play against type, they got it.

By "playing against type," I mean breaking expectations, especially when those expectations are biased and wrong. Examples are a salesperson who cares about the bottom line, with the stereotype of wanting to close a deal at all costs; a lawyer with practical business sense, with the stereotype that lawyers take forever to come up with an answer and the result is wishy-washy when you get it; and an actuary who's a good public speaker, with the stereotype that an extroverted actuary stares at the other person's shoes.

While I know many financially savvy and honest salespeople, several practical and quick lawyers, and a bevy of engaging actuaries, playing against expectations can help.

 *Know your preferences when making career decisions, and focus on your strengths to begin building a positive reputation.* 

Building a Rep

There are other specific actions you can take to help shape your reputation.

I once walked into an annual performance review where my boss, a laconic New Hampshire farmer turned insurance executive, informed me that his boss, Roger, thought I was lazy. After he scraped me off the ceiling, he explained: "I didn't say you were lazy. I said *Roger* thinks you're lazy. Why do you think that is, and what can we do about it?"

Some research uncovered a culprit. I had been in the habit of going to the fitness center each afternoon about 5:00 and coming back up to my desk after a workout. Roger, by contrast, was in the habit of walking the floor at 5:30, adjudging those he found at their desks as hard workers and those who weren't as uncommitted. With some brainstorming, I switched up my workout schedule a few days a week and sent occasional emails, with a copy to Roger, at 7 or 8 p.m.

I ran into Roger one evening in the parking area, and he said, "Go home, Brian. You're working too hard."

If you're aware of how you're perceived, you can manage perceptions of you without altering your values or character.

Another technique for shaping your reputation is to surprise people every once in a while, even if (and maybe because) you seem unreasonable. A team once approached me for approval of a technology project that had started at $200,000 and through multiple revisions grown to their current request for almost four times that amount. It was a critical project, and they presented a cogent argument as to why we needed to do it. My reputation at the time was as a rational investor who saw the logic in efforts and prioritized well but was maybe a little soft on budget, so I shocked them when I said no and stuck to my guns despite their panic that a host of other initiatives depended on this one being completed.

Two days later, they had gotten the cost back down to a reasonable level, but the real benefit wasn't the cost savings on a single project. It was the benefit to my reputation. On every future project that came to me, the team had kicked the tires thoroughly ahead of time because "Brian really cares about the budget."

In at least half of the development conversations I've had with people with potential, I've relayed one more approach to managing reputation: Use headlines. Especially in a group and before giving your reaction or proposal, use a headline to interject why it's important to you first: "The number one thing we need to do this year is improve our relationships with our customers. We haven't been doing enough for them." Then go to the details: "So yes, I approve this upgrade to our call center team's technology so that the customer doesn't have to enter the same information three times before they speak with someone."

In a one-on-one update with a boss or other leader, start by grounding them and getting their attention with a reminder about why the update is important among a dozen other pressing items. Then get to the point, the headline, quickly: "I want to give you an update on the timing of our new product release. As a reminder, it's important because if it doesn't go in on time, we're going to miss our sales plan by twenty percent this year, and that's half of our bonus." This headline approach has repaired the reputation of many people viewed as too mired in detail.

Regardless of which approach you use to manage perceptions, keep the communication going throughout to make sure you understand and are understood. Work hard and do the right thing.

> *Without compromising your character and integrity, you can still manage the perception of your actions.*

When the Exit Sign Is Flashing

If after all your efforts you're unhappy and it's not working out to your satisfaction, move on. The upside of staying someplace for a long time is that you're the survivor and might eventually rise to the top. The downside is that people remember who you were ten or twenty years ago. More than once, a move to a new place has enhanced my reputation, and I found that my voice and experience carried more weight than they did at my prior company.

> *Move on if you need to.*

Wait! I Didn't Mean Me!

Companies use lots of euphemisms for layoffs, including "pink slips," "RIFs (reductions in force)," "downsizing," "right-sizing," "separation from service," or the particularly impersonal "workforce rationalization." At one employer, it became so routine that we just called it "the fall classic." They all hurt.

Having been on the receiving end of this process twice myself, as well as having to communicate loss of a job several times to others, I have a few thoughts.

First and foremost, you will get through it. In every case I remember, even those where I wasn't involved, I've seen people land well, many times in a better spot than the one they left. The change was the impetus they needed to think about what was really important in life.

An important early step is understanding the details. Losing your job often comes as a surprise. I know of one unfortunate person who found out about her dismissal when someone inadvertently left an original HR termination form on the copy machine. In another case, a group was told during a virtual meeting, "If you're in this meeting, you've been let go." However, you don't need such a dramatic revelation to feel overwhelmed. Even if you're sitting across from your boss and/or HR, with one or both available for follow-up, you're likely so shocked and emotional at the moment of impact that you're still processing and not hearing the information that's being provided. Additionally, whoever is on the other side of the table is moving as quickly as they can to get through what they're saying in order to move on to the next person.

A day or two after you've found out that you're leaving, take the time to use the resources available to ask questions and to write down the answers. Go back and confirm your benefits, how long you're still there, what happens to your medical coverage under COBRA, what you have to sign, what it means you're giving up the right to, and anything else you're not sure about.

Here's another consideration, and it's a biggie: It's not your fault.

A job is sometimes so intertwined with our identity that it can be easy to get stuck in self-doubt when you lose it. *What did I do wrong? Why didn't I see this coming? Who was out to get me?* Don't. It's not healthy. If you could see both sides of it, you might learn that you likely didn't do anything wrong. Often it's that those running the company didn't prepare adequately for a change in circumstances.

As with any significant loss, allow yourself the time to process, but don't get stuck in anger. Take action to move on to the next steps, which are deciding what you want to do and looking for a new job. Throw yourself into that. This doesn't mean grabbing the first thing that comes along. Wait for the right opportunity. But if you're going to spend time on introspection, examine what you're really good at and what you like to do rather than debating how you possibly could've changed something that already happened.

Here's one last piece of advice, and please don't ignore it: There are people in your life you trust. Whether that's a spouse or partner, a friend, or your mom, let them remind you how good you are. Then hear it. Most importantly, believe it. Use it to lift yourself up. It's not only okay to accept help and support from others but essential.

 *Use the loss of a job as an opportunity to adjust your career to something better.* 

Summary

You can take steps to steer your career toward the path you want it to take and continually move in the right direction:

- *In searching for a new job, follow up on every opportunity, treat everyone with kindness and respect, and keep in mind their points of view.*

- *When starting a new job, look to create a positive early surprise and visibility. Raise your hand early and often. New job or old, treat every day like it's your first and as if you have to earn the right to be there.*
- *As you think about your career and future opportunities, set a general direction and adjust as needed. Discover what you do and don't like, spend time polishing your strengths, and play against type to stand out.*
- *Consciously shape the reputation you want to have. Be aware of how you're perceived, push back on occasion, and use headlines.*
- *Leave a bad job if you need to.*
- *Use the loss of a job as an opportunity to adjust your career to something better.*

In the Thick of It

Once you're established mid-career, there are common situations and thematic trends that arise again and again, and they often overlap. These chapters cover these recurring specialty areas of focus as you evolve from merely getting the job done to becoming a leader.

- Chapter 6 describes the challenges that can lead to miscommunications, with some suggestions as to how to maintain good communications.
- Chapter 7 provides guidance for making better decisions and prioritizing which ones to make.
- Chapter 8 covers ways to face and overcome challenges and adversity.
- Chapter 9 takes you through process improvements and turnaround situations.
- Chapter 10 is all about motivating individuals and teams.
- Chapter 11 reprises the multi-prong challenge described in the introduction as a case study, along with how the tools in this section were used to solve it.

Chapter 6

Miss Communications

Effective communication is the foundation of both personal and professional relationships, yet it's often fraught with misunderstandings. Whether we're interacting with colleagues or loved ones, the process of exchanging information can be prone to errors at every step. These miscommunications, though often subtle, can lead to confusion, frustration, and even conflict. Understanding the dynamics of communication and recognizing where things can go wrong is key to improving how we connect with others and ensuring that the message we intend to share is the one that's heard.

In this chapter, we'll cover the following questions:

- *What causes miscommunications?*
- *What are some specific types of miscommunication?*
- *What leads to good communication?*
- *What are some techniques a speaker can use to maintain audience engagement?*

Where Do Miscommunications Come From?

I once saw an article in *The Wall Street Journal* premising that long-term couples do in fact grow to look like each other over time. It's not just a myth.

The explanation is that a key element of communication is echoing back to someone to be sure you understand them. We echo not just with words but with facial expressions. Repeat the echoing process enough times with the same facial muscles, and you end up looking like each other. That's how important communication is. It becomes physical!

I am convinced that 90 percent of issues at work arise from miscommunication. I'm still learning but would guess the same is true in personal relationships. It's not surprising after analysis, because even in a single communication there's the potential for error from the sender of a message, by the receiver, and in translation.

Why does it seem that socks go missing so easily? I think I have the answer. We keep socks in pairs. If one is missing, the pair is broken. We don't have to lose them both. If we drop one of two socks on the way from the bedroom to the laundry, we have a mismatch. If we drop one while transferring them from the hamper to the washer, there's another opportunity for a break. From the washer to the dryer is another, from the dryer to folding is another, and from folding to putting them away is yet one more. There's a whole chain of events, and a break at any one point, by either sock, means a mismatch.

The same goes for communication. If either sender or receiver has a misunderstanding, the communication is broken, and it's amplified when there are multiple communications, when time goes by between conversations and people forget (or remember only what they want to hear), and when there are more than two parties involved.

> ***Communication is dependent on a chain
> of events, and any break can cause
> miscommunication.***

I Mean to Say

Sometimes miscommunication can arise from something as fundamental as a difference in definition.

Wrestling through an issue with a Dutch friend and colleague, I suggested we ought to "table" a controversial topic for an upcoming meeting, meaning we should defer it to a later time because we still had several unresolved items. He agreed, then asked whether I should bring up the issue in the meeting or he should. I was confused given I had just suggested the opposite. We had a good laugh when he said that, to him, "tabling" it meant putting it *on the table* for discussion.

During a work trip to Chile, my colleagues and I had a similar definitional misunderstanding. In addition to Chilenos, Argentines, Mexicans, and Colombians in our group describing each other's accents in colorful terms, they also had different words for things. As a baby, our son was affectionately referred to as a *guagua*, a nickname similar to "kiddo" but for an infant. But in some other countries, *guagua* means "bus."

Comparatively, during a site visit for a retirement plan for a Texas border city, we avoided a communications disaster at the last second. We had posters made up in Spanish, translated by a firm in Miami. Florida Spanish is different from Texas Spanish, and in a final preview meeting the city's broker saw the poster with its beautiful graphics well-representing that part of Texas, but he said he didn't recognize half of the words. To make it worse, instead of *ciudad*, meaning "city," the poster welcomed *cuidado*, meaning "danger." We tucked the posters into a cabinet just as our guests arrived.

I learned this lesson again when I boarded with the widower in Wellesley. We got along well but didn't always operate on the same level of understanding. Since I was a young college student and surely must have known about drugs, he asked me one day what an article in the paper meant when it said, "I took a hit of vitamin C before going out the door."

"It means he had a glass of orange juice."

"Oh."

And during that early visit to LA, there was a funny incident at one evening's karate practice. Practitioners from nearby university dojos would often visit the central dojo to receive direct instruction from top instructors. Mr. Ohshima was giving explicit directions to a third-degree black belt after practice, and all the fighter's Caltech buddies were haranguing him and laughing uproariously.

"What happened?" I asked.

"Well, Mr. Ohshima was explaining to Dan that he's been tying his belt wrong for years."

"And why's that so funny?"

"Because Dan is the world's leading expert in a branch of mathematics called 'knot theory.'"

Later, when I moved the family during a time of economic upheaval, we decided to build, watching every penny. I'd stop by the site almost every day to check on progress as the land was cleared, the foundation hole was dug, the foundation was poured, and the walls were erected. Our builder, Andre, was excellent. I've seen him trim a ten-foot piece of siding perfectly straight with a handheld power saw all by eye. In his mid-fifties and wiry, he sported a lyrical, almost mesmerizing Canadian French accent. I stopped by one day and saw him hanging upside down from the rafters in what was to become our master bedroom, pounding nails in by hand to show two younger workers how to do it the right way. I had envisioned what's called a "tray" ceiling, a slightly elevated and angled ceiling appropriate to the largest bedroom in the house, but I changed my mind when I saw how nice the partially completed work looked.

"Say, Andre, do you think you could make this into a cathedral ceiling?" I asked.

He dropped down, dismounting like a gymnast from the rafters, and looked up at his work. "I want to make sure the house is solid," he said, rubbing his chin. "Tell you what. I'll make you a Caesar ceiling."

Wary of cost, I pictured Caesar, the ruler of the Roman Empire at its most opulent, and wondered what kind of ceiling he might have had, probably ornate marble columns supporting gold-encrusted leaves of ivy. "Andre, what exactly is a Caesar ceiling?"

He looked at me as if I were as uninformed as the junior employees he'd been showing the art of nailing to and pointed at the rafters he'd just climbed down from. "You see ze beams?" he asked.

I nodded.

Holding up two fingers, he said, "You see how zay cross in ze meedle, like a pair of seezers?"

We can understand each other. We just need to work at it, both as listeners and speakers.

> *Miscommunication can be as simple as using different language and definitions. Check with others to be sure you're understood and that you understand them.*

Assume the Position

Even when definitions are commonly understood, miscommunication can arise from a difference in intent.

Our karate group had a "special training" a few times a year, and the summer ones were especially challenging. At my first, I learned we'd be waking up early, running a couple of miles barefoot, and practicing several times a day for four days straight, returning from each one exhausted. The most intense of all the practices is *kiba dachi*, or horse stance, a bear even for experienced practitioners. You walk into the gym after wiping the dewy grass off your feet from the run, notice all the clocks are covered, and feel the buzz of nervous energy that comes with anticipation. You then line up in concentric circles facing inward, with the top candidate for *Sandan*, third-level black belt, in the center for everyone to key off of. On the command to begin, you crouch into stance and stand, legs bent, for ninety minutes.

But it doesn't take more than a few of those minutes before your legs start to hurt and shake. Someone comes up behind you and pokes at the back of your knee with their foot, commanding, "Lower! Push!" When the last ten minutes or so arrive, you can feel it. After a crescendo of *kiais*, or yelling, the person in the center yells "*Yame!*" (Stop!), and somehow you stagger to an upright position, waiting for the final command to be at ease. You cool down, mop up the sweat, massage your legs, and try to walk.

That was the morning practice the day Sensei Ohshima flew in from California. Then in the afternoon, with the same legs we'd stood on for ninety minutes in the morning, we did a one thousand-kick practice, after which I stumbled back to the dorms to find Sensei sitting on a wall, signing copies of our training manual.

Because hierarchy is everything in karate, we, as white belts, were all up on the fourth floor. After I literally pulled myself up the stairs using the handrail to get my copy before he left, I managed to drag it back downstairs to the courtyard to ask if he'd sign it. He did, starting with "Dear Brian."

Then he wrote a message in Japanese *kanji* characters. I was overwhelmed that our chief instructor had written me a personal message of inspiration. Expectantly I asked, "Sensei, what does it say?"

"June 17, 1979."

 **Watch out for assumptions in communications.** 

Working for a Bigwig

Miscommunication can also stem from a difference in perspective.

One of my governmental visits was with the State of Missouri, and our team flew to St. Louis, then drove from there to Jefferson City, the capital, to see whether we might put in a bid on Missouri's plan and to meet with a consultant to prepare.

My mom, hearing I was traveling to her home state where we still had many relatives, suggested I look up her cousin. "She's a secretary there," she said.

"Mom. How am I going to find one secretary out of all the people who work at the capitol?"

"Well, she's a secretary for one of the bigwigs. Somebody might know her."

So, we spent the day with the consultant, including hearing a story from him about how some bureaucratic process had resulted in the state buying an unnecessary second helicopter because the one previously purchased didn't have the serial number identified in the purchase order. We decided not to bid.

Saying goodbye in the parking lot, I asked the consultant if he knew my family member who was a secretary for one of the bigwigs.

"What's her name?" he asked. "I might know her. I know a lot of the secretaries."

I told him, and he hooted.

"She works for one of the bigwigs alright. The governor."

That sounded impressive.

He chuckled some more and said, "She's the Secretary of State."

> **Be clear on the reference point of the person you're gathering information from.**

Decreasing Signal Strength

Sometimes miscommunication is due to the telephone game effect, the cumulative misinterpretation of multiple communications in a chain.

I was meeting with my team in Florida when I decided on a particular course of action. My team shook their heads.

"We can't do it that way."

"Why not?"

"I don't know. I just know some senior person said we're not allowed to."

I was angry now. We were finally starting to make progress cleaning things up. "We get back together Thursday. Somebody here is going to find out who's saying we can't do this. I want a name, and I will personally talk with them and get it done." I waved my hand. "Go."

When we were back together, I asked, "Well, who was it that said we can't do it?"

My team was laughing.

"What?"

"Well," pipes up one, "according to our research, it was you."

Someone had taken something I'd said, the exact opposite position of the alleged prohibition, and by the time it worked its way through the organization it had transformed into the inverse.

> **Be especially wary of communication that makes its way through multiple people or is ascribed to no one in particular.**

Buzz, Buzz

In one of Clayton Christensen's books on innovation, he describes the importance of a novelty that those of us who grew up with landlines probably took for granted: the dial tone. Before its invention, when we picked up the phone to make a call, we had no feedback that indicated it was working. In a house like ours with a party line, a dial tone let us know whether we could make a call or Mom needed to send me next door to ask the neighbors to free up the phone.

While a critical component of communication is listening, as in the previous stories in this chapter, doing so may not be enough in and of itself. Echoing back to ensure understanding can help: "Let me make sure I understood you correctly." Similarly, since communication is bidirectional, it may be worth repeating important points with different language.

There may be a risk in either case, such as coming across as slow or implying that the other person hasn't heard you, but if you approach both sides with positive intent, the clarification is almost always worth the risk.

Work to understand and to be understood.

On the Edge of Your Seat

I once stumbled on a speaker's trick by accident.

Upon landing exhausted in the US after a trip to Latin America, I rushed to emcee an awards dinner for a symphony conductor, a neighborhood revitalizer, and a reformed gang member and prison inmate who was working to keep kids out of trouble. Startling the organizer by going immediately off the script I'd been provided, I described how I'd just traveled through three of the largest cities in the world in three days and the common connections I'd noticed between them. But I forgot to mention the names of the three cities.

This turned out to be fortuitous. In the donors' lounge after the event, several people approached me and said, "I kept listening to every word. I wanted to know what the three cities were." This taught me that if you set up a problem or question or only part of a story at the inception of your remarks, people will be dying to know the answer. That's been a useful technique in many of my presentations ever since.

Another approach that works when speaking with groups is to tell a story. Asked in one session how best to tell one, I explained that it's really up to the individual but suggested telling only the truth, to relate a story that's meaningful to you, and, although it's your story, to remember that you're telling it for the benefit of the audience rather than to show off. Pressed further, I provided one sample structure from among many:

1. Start by describing the environment, emotional or physical.
2. Describe a problem you faced; the more challenging, the better.
3. What failed attempts did you make to solve the problem?
4. What solution did you finally land on?
5. What was the result?

That's one way, but adapt these points to you.

> ***Invite curiosity from your listeners to maintain engagement.***

Oh, and if you're still paying attention, the three cities were New York, Sao Paolo, and Mexico City.

Summary

It's easy to miscommunicate, and miscommunication comes from multiple sources. Good communication is hard and takes work, but it's worth the effort.

- ***Any break in the chain of communication can cause a problem.***

> - *Miscommunication can arise from differences in definition, intent, assumption, and perspective.*
> - *Be especially wary of communication that involves multiple parties or is secondhand.*
> - *Ensure understanding in both directions. Repeat as necessary.*
> - *Establish curiosity in a communication or presentation to enhance engagement.*

Chapter 7

Decision-Making
and Prioritization

We make hundreds of decisions a day, some simple and others complex and seemingly insurmountable. As we're debating a decision, every fact appears important, every consequence likely, and every option the act of giving something up. This biases our objective assessment. There are some specific tools and techniques to step away from that bias, and to make better decisions.

In this chapter, we'll cover the following questions:

- *What specific techniques work well to improve decision-making?*
- *How can I change my perspective when I make decisions?*
- *How can I distance myself and remain objective when necessary?*
- *How should I prioritize my decision-making?*
- *How do I follow up once I make a decision?*

As If!

One of our senior karate instructors, who when younger was the top kickboxer in France, once explained to our class how to attack more quickly: "You have to make the decision to fight *before* the

---

105

fight starts, not during it. You are a strung arrow, ready to fly. You're already committed. The decision about *whether* to strike is already made. The only remaining decision is *when*."

An example that comes to mind is when a former friend and colleague facing a hiring decision struggled with deciding between two candidates. She'd put together an extensive list of pros and cons, and since either could've done the job there was no downside, yet she debated herself for ninety minutes. I finally said, "I think you should hire A."

"Why?"

I walked through my rationale, and she got ready to go ahead on that basis. I then seemed to waver. "Wait. I think you should hire B."

Clearly growing frustrated by my change in direction, she again asked why. After listing my reasons for the switch, I asked which of the two arguments she'd just heard was more compelling. Her decision became easy: "I like them both, but I need help right away, so I'm going with A."

> *By treating a decision as having already been made, argumentation takes on a different tone, and you don't have a sense of loss.*

Substitute

That sense of loss, or loss aversion, is innate in humans. In behavioral finance terms, it's described as the "endowment effect," meaning we assign more value to something we own than to something we don't.

One of many famous experiments on this effect involved dividing a group of students into two, with half receiving a cheap ceramic mug upon entry to the classroom. When students without a mug were asked how much they would spend to acquire one, their answer was much lower than the willing sale price of those students who'd been gifted one.

A similar phenomenon applies to a position in an argument and even to a political belief. Once you lock into it, every fact you see supports your position (confirmation bias), and you become increasingly less willing to see the other side. We hate to give up something once we have it.

So here's the trick: When making a decision and you hear yourself using the phrase "giving up," replace it with "trading up." For instance, instead of "giving up" the old car you love with 150,000 miles on it, you're "trading up" for a new one and the excitement that comes with it. Or at work, instead of "I'm giving up this project I've been working on for two years," replace it with "I'm trading up to a project with much better likelihood of success."

A related technique is to list the pros of two options rather than both the pros and the cons. Focus on the positives. Then, once you've made your decision on that basis, treat the decision as if it has already been made ("as if"), ask what could go wrong, and plan how to react to those negatives. Thinking through potential negatives as secondary considerations rather than as components of your decision incites protective action subsequent to the decision rather than polluting your decision process with inaction because of what bad things might happen.

Another technique I've both used and advised comes from Katy Milkman, a brilliant professor of behavioral economics at the Wharton School. In an episode of her podcast *Choiceology*, she talks about asking ourselves what advice we'd give a friend who's making a similar decision. By moving the impact of our decision away from us personally and notionally putting it onto someone else, we're more evenhanded and put less weight on the loss.

> *When making a decision, try to remove or distance yourself from the sense of loss and focus on what you're likely to gain.*

First Things First: A Structured Approach

I don't like prioritizing because it feels like I'm giving something up. But we must let go of certain things to trade up, to excel at what we choose to do. Relying on structure helps.

Grandma's Rule is certainly one useful technique for prioritization, but it can be a blunt instrument. For more thoughtful prioritization, consider ranking projects or initiatives using a matrix. I've seen at least a dozen different prioritization matrices, and they can all be useful. A simple one that has worked well for me is based on importance and urgency. Importance measures how crucial a task is, and urgency determines how quickly it needs to be done. You score each task in importance from 1–5 in both categories, multiply the scores to determine where to focus your time, then rank each task accordingly. Here's an example using household tasks:

Sample Prioritization Matrix

Project	A: Impact	B: Urgency	Score (A x B)	Ranking
Buy Dinner	3	5	15	2
Plan Next Year's Vacation	4	2	8	4
Fix Brakes	5	5	25	1
Pick Up Laundry	2	5	10	3

A critical project should start now, even if it takes time, while a lower-priority project should rank higher if it must be completed soon to meet a release schedule or support other projects.

Regardless of which approach you use, remember that any algorithm is only a guideline for discussion. Maintain the freedom to vary from what the approach is suggesting. If your instincts are sending you in a different direction from a matrix ranking, don't ignore the disconnect or throw out the matrix. Ask why there's a difference, and you're likely to discover an insight into what's really driving your prioritization.

One use for this simplified importance–urgency matrix is for maintaining an ongoing to-do list. One word of warning, though, is to limit short-term lists to relatively few items, otherwise you'll likely become overwhelmed by how much work is ahead of you.

Sometimes decision-making is a group exercise, and gathering buy-in from others during the prioritization process, especially those who'll be responsible for the work of implementing decisions, is as or more important than the actual decision itself. In this case, a more detailed approach that allows for some debate and discussion can be helpful. I've used an expanded version of the importance–urgency approach successfully with large groups to decide which sales prospects to pursue, which initiatives to prioritize within a budget, which new innovation initiatives to fund, and which businesses to keep or shut down.

One memorable use was with an indecisive nonprofit. We met three times to set their five-year strategy, with different attendees each time, and it worked. The first step was to get everyone to agree on success, what objectives they were aiming for, and which benefits they were seeking. This organization identified three: financial stability, community impact (especially on kids), and positive pub-licity. Next, we brainstormed over one hundred potential initiatives without ranking them, then scored each on how well it aligned with the objectives and how expensive and challenging it would be to implement. Importantly, we emphasized that people could change their minds, though they rarely did.

Graphing the results almost always produces three categories:

1. "Let's do it"—tasks that are easy to execute and high-impact
2. "On-deck"—projects that missed the mark but might be tweaked for later (helpful to avoid a sense of loss)
3. "Don't do it"—initiatives that shouldn't be pursued, often including someone's pet project

Here's what it looks like:

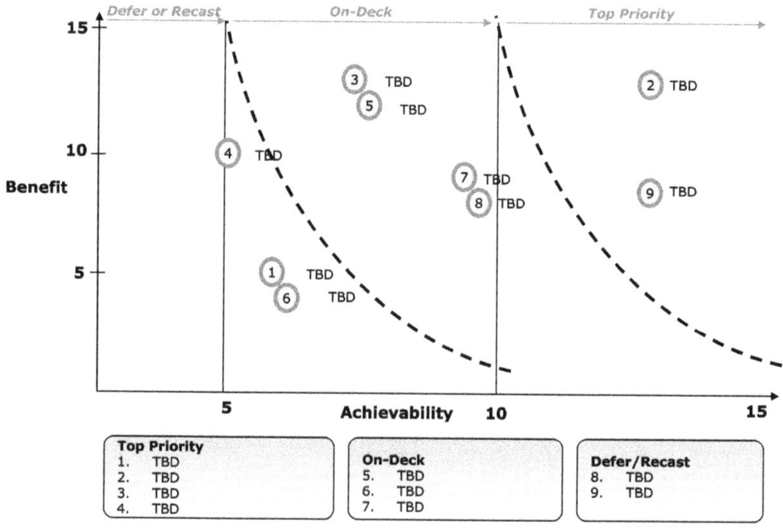

For the nonprofit, one initiative they'd been close to writing a check for was bringing Colin Powell to speak at the city's civic center. Powell was an inspiring speaker, but when we ranked the event, it fell into the unattractive category, primarily because of financial risk. If they couldn't fill the venue, they'd blow their budget and risk going under. To fill the space, they would need corporate sponsors, but that would likely lead to a crowd of corporate attendees instead of the local kids they hoped to impact. Realizing this, they switched tactics, opting for a local celebrity who volunteered to speak and limiting attendance to students, their parents, and the media. This approach better aligned with their goals.

 *Use structure and process as useful guides for prioritization.* 

Not Done Yet

Choosing priorities, whether quickly or through an extended process, is just the first step in making a decision. Execution is key, and structure can ensure execution as well as clarify the decisions you make.

One example is to establish limits, boundaries, or dedicated time. Especially with a group, setting aside dedicated time to review status, even when it doesn't feel like it's needed, forces the team to come together, check on progress, and adjust as necessary.

You can use the same approach to manage your own capacity to focus on your most important priorities. For example, I set aside a few minutes at the end of each day or an hour at the end of the week to prioritize upcoming work, and some excellent executive assistants blocked out meetings the first hour or two of a return from travel.

I knew staying connected with my team was critical, so I also scheduled time in my calendar every couple of weeks dedicated to walking around the floor. If I didn't schedule it, it disappeared. By scheduling it, it had priority. And when my investments processing team found themselves deep underwater as we transitioned from calculating and posting 10,000 values a night to 120,000, two of my key employees designated office hours for people to come by and ask questions, freeing the remainder of their time to stay on task.

It can also be useful to set the time at which you go home. It's hard at first. A simple technique is to say goodbye to your desk at the end of a day or week and acknowledge that the work will be there when you get back. Often, the issue you would've stayed late to work on will have gone away by the time you return.

One other useful tool to ensure follow-through is to pair yourself with an execution freak. There are people in most organizations who have a different mentality than most and are good at establishing limits, providing updates, and forcing decisions. I once had a good friend approach me at work to suggest that I do exactly that because "It's hard for people to track everything you've got going on." When I initially balked, arguing that I had everything in my head, she let me know that was the problem—it was in my head, and no one could see it.

I hired an excellent, organized execution freak who set up regular team meetings on all our initiatives. The prior year, we'd pushed through four, but with her help we managed forty.

 *__Prioritization is not a one-and-done process. It's constant. Use structure to ensure ongoing execution and adjustment.__* 

Summary

Decision-making can benefit from specific techniques and structure, both of which help us overcome innate human biases:

- *Use the "as if" framework, treating a decision as if it has already been made.*
- *Replace the phrase "giving up" with "trading up."*
- *Make your decision based on the positives, and consider negatives only after the decision is made.*
- *To distance yourself from the decision, think about how you'd advise a friend.*
- *Use a prioritization matrix.*
- *Once made, set limits and dedicate time to following through on the decision, and adjust as necessary.*

Chapter 8

Dealing with Challenges
or Adversity

In aphorism number 8 of the "Maxims and Arrows" section of his 1888 book The Twilight of the Idols, philosopher Friedrich Nietzsche writes, "Was mich nicht umbringt, macht mich stärker," which translates roughly to "What doesn't destroy me, makes me stronger." And in his book Antifragile, Nassim Nicholas Taleb espouses a concept of building strength through the gradual introduction of greater and greater stresses, using as examples the annealing of metal (twist, turn, and stress it to make it stronger), running a new engine at slow and fast speeds to break it in (rather than just one constant speed), exposing your kids to problems of increasing difficulty and responsibility, and even varying diet to stay healthy. In a similar vein, in karate training it's the senior's responsibility to bring out the best in the juniors, to give them as much as they can handle but not enough to break them. Managed the right way, adversity can be a source of development and strength.

In this chapter, we'll cover the following questions:

- *How can I assess a challenge before diving into dealing with it?*
- *How does the gradual introduction of stress build protection against adversity?*

- *Can knowledge help with adversity?*
- *How much can relationships help?*
- *What's the value of persistence?*
- *How do I deal with imposter syndrome?*
- *Should I face a challenge head-on?*

In the Frame

One tool that helps when you confront adversity is how you look at it. Remember that a challenge is an opportunity to learn and grow. More than once during especially busy times, I've reminded teams, "We're going to get about three years' worth of knowledge out of the next six months" and have watched those folks who looked at it that way rise in the organization shortly afterward.

In his book *David and Goliath*, Malcolm Gladwell describes adversity as not just an opportunity to learn but a prerequisite to innovation. David couldn't take on Goliath through traditional means. He had to use a slingshot so Goliath wouldn't take his head off in close-quarters combat.

Does a problem feel too big? Chunk it up into pieces so that you can celebrate small successes and important moments and maintain the sense of progress we all crave. Similarly, focus on what's most important. By letting a few lesser priorities wait until later, you can focus on the most crucial areas first.

Also, focus on what you can control. Investment and retirement companies struggled mightily after the 2008 global financial crisis because their revenues declined with the markets while their expenses didn't, and profits turned into losses. Confronted with a question about why we were bothering to tighten budgets when it wouldn't be enough to cover damage from down markets, our president replied simply, "Because it's what we can control."

> **Frame challenges in a way that helps you best address them.**

Read the Board

Awareness is another important component of developing adversity management skills.

In an annual intracompany chess championship, I seemed to find myself each year playing in the final match against Sergei, a technology developer who spent two years at a Russian chess school. In a tiebreaker in one of those finals, I'd gotten ahead early using a tactic and should've been able to bring home the point in a pretty straightforward way. Several moves later, I made a mistake and found myself fighting hard just to get back to even. In the middle of chastising myself for the mistake, I realized I couldn't take back a move or go back to a previous position. I had to play with the assets I still had.

That's one of the things about adversity—it forces you to assess what you *do* have. In chess, absent an outright blunder, you usually have a compensating advantage. You might give up material, but you picked up control of space, development, or better pawn structure. You play to those strengths, which you might not even have noticed if you hadn't made the mistake.

Though I was fortunate enough to win that game (but only after Sergei graciously didn't fault me for violating a touch-move rule), subsequent computer analysis showed not only that both of us had made many more mistakes than either of us realized but also that neither of us was fully aware of each other's assets.

> ***In assessing a challenge or a setback, pay attention to the strengths and assets you have, not just what you're at risk of losing.***

One More Rep!

The Outward Bound program I described in chapter 3 is known for its experiential learning and in such diverse and daunting areas as sea kayaking and rock climbing. I learned from an instructor that the program's origins are rooted in overcoming adversity.

In World War II, the British navy was losing too many sailors to German U-boat torpedoes. Although some sailors abandoned ship, many perished in the cold waters of the North Atlantic while awaiting rescue. Curiously, more older sailors survived than the presumably stronger and healthier younger ones. Upon interviewing each, many younger sailors mentioned having contemplated their imminent demise just before rescue, while older salts often said things like, "I've been through tough times before. I knew somebody would come along and pull us out." Thus began the Navy's program of introducing graduated stress to build resilience in the face of adversity, and Outward Bound echoed this approach in a private company.

A simple exercise involved overcoming a fear of heights, first by participants standing atop a six-inch hewed-down piece of telephone pole, then gradually increasing the height until they stood balancing on one leg on top of a thirty-foot pole, then bending to pick up an object at their feet before jumping off in a safety harness to celebrate.

For my group, the challenge was a tightrope walk, where we linked arms and leaned back in opposite directions to balance together as we crossed high up between trees. The final challenge was spending a night solo in the woods. While many city dwellers close to the cabin were unsettled by the night sounds, I had a peaceful experience deep in the forest, waking only once to a sky full of stars and a bright moon before discovering in the morning that I'd slept through a nighttime visit from a moose.

The most significant transformation came from a former football player, gang member, and entrepreneur turned preacher. He'd developed a deep fear of water due to a traumatic childhood experience in which a gym teacher had thrown him into a pool to teach him to swim. During our initial canoe trip he was terrified, but through gradual encouragement and familiarity he gained confidence. Days later, after a hike, he submerged his head in water for the first time in over thirty years, a breakthrough that brought him to tears at our graduation and marked his triumph over fear and adversity.

 *You can build resilience through gradually introducing stresses and challenges.* 

What Do You Know?

One challenge of switching jobs is that most things are new and unfamiliar.

When after half a dozen years in Maine my wife and I moved to Connecticut to be closer to family, I started a new product development job with a much larger company. It was like moving to the big leagues. There was a larger campus to navigate, many more employees, new people to get to know, experts around every corner, and, naturally, a whole new culture and business to learn.

In Maine we had rolled out a new product every year or two, but in Connecticut the initial list of new efforts in flight had thirty-three items, many of them cutting edge for Fortune 100 clients. There was a lot to pick up fast.

An early assignment was to create efficiency by merging three investment vehicles called "separate accounts," all invested in short-term debt, an important area at the time given high interest rates. I didn't know what separate accounts were, how they worked, what they invested in, or what law applied, so I did the only thing I could think of: I asked a lot of questions. Feeling like a cross between a detective and a talk show host, I interrogated the investment team, cajoled answers from actuaries and lawyers, and even sat with the short-term traders at their desks as they talked with their counterparts on Wall Street. A seasoned lawyer called my resulting report the "hornbook," a sort of CliffsNotes, on short-term investing.

What I discovered in this exercise and saw repeated many times afterward is that while people know a lot about their individual areas, they often don't know about the interactions among other parts of the company. A more complex effort, for example, was to develop a single product that could be used by lots of different types of investors, such as institutional retirement plans, foundations and endowments, and nuclear decommissioning trusts. This time, in addition to consulting resources inside the company, I met with state insurance departments, the DOL, the IRS (who had a professor there on loan), the SEC, and the DOJ.

Afterward, when sharing the successful new product that resulted from these meetings with the divisional president, a fiery Irishman with a penchant for colorful language and imagery, I was proud that through Herculean effort we'd delivered a month early against his April deadline, only to hear a surprise: "Oh! I didn't really t'ink you'd get it done by April. I needed it by June. I've learned to ask for t'ings early here if ya want 'em on time."

Wasted effort? Not at all. I learned a lot and developed a reputation for delivering on difficult and complex initiatives.

My newly acquired skill of persistent questioning was invaluable on a personal level when my father-in-law was diagnosed with Alzheimer's. I'd moved in temporarily with my wife's folks while she finished up work in Maine, and we soon noticed her incredibly intelligent father failing to retrieve the necessary words to complete a sentence. When he complained about problems with his investments, I looked them over, and it was worse than I could've imagined. He'd made the wise choice to take a lump-sum early retirement from a steel company about to go bankrupt, but an unscrupulous broker had taken advantage of his declining cognition and churned his account, losing all of his retirement assets in inappropriate investments in the 1987 stock market crash and leaving the family owing a small fortune to the brokerage firm.

His decline was further confirmed when first the bank called and asked that he stop visiting daily to ask where his money was when his balance was under a dollar, and I went through his bill drawer to find that he'd been approved for eighteen credit cards and maxed them all out. When an incident at home sparked the immediate need for a diagnosis, the search for information this time included several doctors, one of whom, a top neurologist, evaluated and diagnosed him, then temporarily committed him to the hospital while we hunted for a facility. After stays at multiple locations, one of which he walked out of and wandered the streets of Hartford, we found excellent care, better than any he'd received in a private facility, at a VA hospital for which he was eligible as an active World War II Navy vet.

Then we got to work on repairing finances. My dad-in-law could still identify the current president and year and was able to transfer home ownership to his wife. We sought out an attorney to sue the brokerage firm, and we settled. The Consumer Credit Counseling Service negotiated discounted payoff amounts on the credit cards, which I funded out of our savings.

The hospital where he had stayed for a month then sent a bill for $80,000. I worked through multiple calls with his insurer and was floored to receive a call from an exultant rep with whom I'd built up a first-name relationship: "You won't believe it, Brian! They paid it!"

We got my mother-in-law to group sessions for Alzheimer's caregivers, sold her house, and ensconced her in a condominium where she wouldn't have to arrange for plowing or lawn service, and where she spent several happy years, including time with her first grandbaby.

I was incredibly thankful to have learned how to find things out.

> *Be dogged in asking questions until you find answers that work.*

Raise Your Hand

In chapter 3, I advocated the technique of throwing yourself into something when you're unfamiliar with it. One of the benefits of doing this when you're confronted with a challenge is that you're still too naive to understand what can't be done when older, more experienced hands give up (more on this in chapter 14).

I was in a large meeting with the head of the division. For months his top salesperson had been negotiating with a large oil company on a price for a new international stock fund in which, if we won, we'd be investing in nineteen countries around the world and pulling off the largest deal of its kind to date.

The division head was complaining because every time we acquiesced to what the customer asked for, they asked for more. This didn't seem complex to me. *Why don't we just tell them no, and they'll know we've gone as low as we can?* I thought. But the division head characterized such brinksmanship as a loss of face.

After a heated discussion that included one of his twenty or so cronies removing his shoe and pounding it on the table like Nikita Khrushchev, he made a decision. "I think we should walk away," he said. "We don't want to do this, unless any of you want to work with Kim [our salesperson] to see if we can come to a deal." I looked around the room as everyone else agreed with him, then, like a kid with virtually no experience who therefore believes anything is possible, I volunteered.

Kim and I messaged back that our current offer was final, and we got the deal done and the contract signed three months later. Naivete had paid off.

But there was one new challenge in a last-minute hitch.

Because the transaction took place across nineteen countries, it was subject to multiple international laws. In particular, we'd gotten legal opinions in both the UK and Hong Kong validating our approach. Half an hour before the transaction was to be effected, we got a call from the British lawyer, who spoke in such a deep, posh, Churchill-like rumble that we pictured him half buried in a burgundy leather armchair twice his size, smoke drifting from a pipe. He advised us that perhaps we should consider pulling the transaction. Upon further analysis, he said there was a risk that the Stamp Act of 1765, the very one that caused upstart Boston colonials to toss tea overboard near the inception of our country, might apply to our arrangement and incur our client a tax.

We reached the customer ten minutes before the deal was to go live and found only two lower-level employees who paralleled my naivete and optimism. Though they had no signing authority, we all decided to complete the transaction. No tax was applied, but I've never tried so hard to will a decision to completion.

> ***When confronting a challenge, be aware of self-imposed limitations.***

Blue Skies and Red Flags

Relying on those relationships you or your colleagues have built is another tool for overcoming challenges.

One Monday, I was called into the big boss's office, where he sat with the head of sales, Billy. Both had just returned from a trip to the nation's largest exporter. "I'm going to describe to you what we sold them," they said.

"Ok," I responded, wondering what the catch was.

"Well, it doesn't exist yet. We need you to build it."

Following a trip to their West Coast headquarters, during which I watched the company treasurer and his wife warmly embrace Billy, we secured the company's approval and built the new product. We did so by asking lots of questions, reverse-engineering and improving a competitor's design, and scheduling a final negotiating session with a bevy of top executives on both sides.

Billy took me and one of our lawyers aside before the meeting and said, "Okay. If [my counterpart] uses the word 'blue,' then they're just blowing smoke and they'll give in on that provision, no matter how loud they get. They just need to look good. If he says 'flag,' we've got to agree to it or they walk away. Same thing going the other direction."

Sure enough, about ten minutes in, Billy's counterpart described a ranting higher-up as "blue in the face." Despite the apparent rancor, we knew we could hold our position. On the other hand, the other side had to "run something up the flagpole and see what it looks like" on one issue and "weren't about to put up the white flag of surrender" on another, and we knew what we had to trade.

The deal was done before we got on the phone.

That's when we had to add persistence to relationships. With the product built and terms agreed on by both parties, we needed approval from the New York insurance department, one of the most difficult regulators in the country, especially for new concepts. We leveraged an obscure "desk drawer" provision to temporarily bypass New York's objection that the product wasn't covered by existing regulation, after which we convened and did shuttle negotiations with a group of industry experts with widely differing agendas and opinions. Then we testified before key decision-makers and essentially wrote the new industry regulation.

After a difficult reporter-filled session during which I debated New York's superintendent of insurance and he turned us down, we continued to build relationships with the multiple layers of regulators under him, biding our time. A change in administration later ousted the superintendent from office, and we brought his replacement up to speed.

Finally, four years after agreeing to terms with the customer, right before Christmas and with no one else left in the office other than me packing up to go home, the phone rang. It was Len, who at age ninety-six was the longest-serving actuary in New York, calling from his home, in a blizzard. "I thought you'd want to know before the new year. They really put you through the wringer on this one, but you're approved."

I thanked him profusely.

"Better get home," he continued. "Not only does your wife need to see you this time of year, but once the blizzard hits, you're not going to be able to drive in it."

I left several happy voice messages and went home.

> ***Relationships are a valuable tool
> for overcoming challenges.***

The Part That's 99 Percent Perspiration

One series of incidents illustrates the combined benefit of asking questions, maintaining naive optimism, leveraging relationships, and being persistent. It also smacks of seemingly surreal coincidences.

A friend and colleague named Michal, now CEO of a Czech insurer, invited me to speak at a conference in Brazil, where he was trying to get a bank into the retirement savings business. I agreed to a short trip, meeting the first day with a group of consultants and brokers, speaking on the second day, then flying to Mexico City to do some consulting.

In Brazil, where consumers still remembered the ravages of hyperinflation, the topic of retirement savings was potentially controversial. Accordingly, to prepare for any tough questions I asked my friend Emily to translate a preliminary copy of the program from Portuguese. She read me the main topic I was slated to address, then bios for the speakers. When she read the last name of one of my co-panelists, I interrupted and asked her to repeat it. It was very familiar but from an unusual connection.

In 1992, when my wife and I traveled to Chile to adopt the first of our two children, an overbooked flight landed us a free upgrade to business class, where I struck up a late-night, post-dinner conversation with a Chilean seatmate. He and his wife had visited the US to pick up their daughter, who had just "donated a year of her life" to a Rhode Island convent. After visiting their home, we started to get a sense of his status when his wife started laughing as he stepped out of the Mercedes and struggled to withdraw money from an ATM.

"What's so funny?" I wondered.

"He owns the bank."

We found out later that evening that he also provides 2 percent of the world's tomato seed crop; supplies grapes, avocados, and other fruits and veggies to US markets; owns a molybdenum mine; and has a ten-thousand-hectare ranch in the south with a volcano on it. In the early 1900s, one of his ancestors was the president.

We maintained correspondence, and the relationship led to another surprise in 1995, when we returned to adopt our daughter. To make this trip a bit of a vacation and adventure, in addition to visiting a local ski resort and practicing karate with the locals, I badged my way past several security guards and half a dozen assistants to meet Sergio, the president of our Chilean operations in Santiago. Staring at me, likely wondering why I was there and what I wanted, he asked, "Who do you know in Chile?"

He shook his head when I gave the social worker's name and nodded when I gave that of our attorney. "Yes," he confirmed. "She used to be on our supreme court. She decided some eminent domain cases that were important to us."

I then mentioned the one other person I knew there, Pancho (or more properly, Don Francisco), the millionaire farmer we'd met solely due to an unscheduled airline seat change. Sergio's eyes widened, he grinned, and in a low, confidential, and deliberate tone he let me know a childhood nickname he'd been calling Don Francisco since they'd grown up together in a tiny town outside the city.

This was why I jumped up from my chair when Emily repeated the name of my fellow panelist in Sao Paolo, causing her to take a step back. Of the handful of people I knew in South America, I was a co-panelist with Sergio, now a consultant for the Chilean government on savings policy, in yet a third country.

Two weeks later, excited for a reunion and thinking I was fully prepared, I arrived at the Hartford airport for my evening flight. That's where the challenges started.

The agent gladly accepted and okayed my passport but then asked for my visa for travel to Brazil. I explained that I was sure my travel department would've told me if I'd needed one. She checked with her supervisor, who emerged from the back smiling and said, "You can get on the plane without a visa if you want to, but I wouldn't. You won't get through Immigration, and they'll just put you on the next plane back."

I called Michal and let him know the bad news. I also checked the requirements for a visa. The process of obtaining one through the Brazilian consulate is complex and comes with several requirements, and normal turnaround is five to six weeks. Michal said he knew a few people at the consulate in New York and that if I wanted to try, we'd see if I could get one the next day, skip the meeting with the consultants, and fly out the following evening.

I booked a ticket on the last train to Manhattan out of New Haven, leaving late that evening. In the interim, I booked a hotel not far from the consulate and called my boss, telling him what had happened. I also let him know that one of the requirements was a letter from an officer of the company, on company letterhead, taking responsibility for my behavior while in Brazil. I told him I was heading into the office and would be writing up an endorsement and forging his signature on it.

That done, I drove to New Haven just in time to catch the train, arriving in New York well after midnight. I awoke early the next morning to purchase required money orders, then waited two and a half hours in line to plead my case with the agent. She put up her hand to stop me as a bike courier, flashing a smirk at me that I interpreted as "I'm way more important than you," cut the line and chatted casually with her for another half hour.

When the courier finally left, flashing the same smirk at me as he had when he came in, I approached the agent again and tried the method Cialdini referenced in *Influence*. I provided a reason, and I was nice: "I know this is going to be a challenge, but I was wondering if there's any way I could get a visa later today so that I can speak at an important conference tomorrow."

Perhaps taken aback at such a brazen request, she didn't laugh in my face, but she did say that she'd never heard of what's normally a month-and-a-half-long process being shortened to a few hours. I could return after the lunch break to find out.

Understanding my odds were low, I nevertheless waited outside the office so that I'd be one of the first in, exchanging updates with Michal in Brazil in the meantime. As I stepped up once more after the break, the courier again cut in, only to look crestfallen when this time the agent flashed the stop motion at *him* and beckoned me forward. "I don't know who you know," she said, "but I've been instructed to get rid of you as quickly as I can so that your people will stop harassing my boss."

Relationships pay off. She processed my papers, asked me to wait while they were printed, stamped, and signed, then delivered them to me just before she closed the window for the day. I thanked her repeatedly before sprinting to a waiting car to avoid the hassle of finding a cab at rush hour, only to end up sitting in traffic and reaching LaGuardia just thirty minutes prior to my scheduled departure.

At first I thought myself lucky finding my flight delayed, but when it happened twice more, I snagged the last seat on the only other flight to Sao Paulo that evening, seconds before my original showed up on the screen as canceled. I raced to the gate, where I received sarcastic applause as I boarded and they closed the door behind me. Not having had time beforehand, I worked on my speech through the night, twisted myself into knots to change into a suit in the plane's bathroom, and stared out the window at dawn rising over the endless sprawl of Sao Paolo.

Neither Immigration nor Customs returned me to the US, and I met my driver, who inched forward for two hours even though we were on a five-lane highway. Michal, in a bit of a panic, met me at the hotel, led me down the escalator to the lower level, and translated the announcer's introduction of our panel as he pushed me through the door. "You're on."

I walked to the stage as if I'd been standing in the back waiting for hours, leaped up the steps to greet Sergio and the other panelists, and delivered one of my best presentations ever, translated into four languages. Even the Q&A with reporters shoving microphones into my face afterward felt routine after the nonstop craziness of the last day and a half.

That evening on the way back to the airport, the cabbie spoke enough English to chat with me, and when I recognized the name of the conference on his radio and asked him what they were saying about it, he said that the Minister of Finance had spoken at it. That's why there had been so much press. He was on the panel right after mine.

By the time I boarded my flight to Mexico, I'd been in Brazil for a total of fifteen hours. I wouldn't have gotten there at all if not for asking lots of questions about what was needed to get a visa, naively assuming I'd be able to get one, leveraging Michal's relationships, and staying persistent in finding ways to get there.

> ***Persistence is another tool to overcome challenges, and it pairs well with other techniques.***

Good Enough

I'm sure you've heard of imposter syndrome, the feeling that you're not good enough to do your job. Maybe you've even experienced it, since it happens at all levels within an organization.

In an interesting juxtaposition, I've found that most people who occasionally question their value are actually good at what they do, acknowledge what they don't know, and continue to grow, while those who are brashly confident are unaware of their lack of knowledge.

So how do you confront those times when you doubt yourself? One way is to look for reinforcement, both from yourself and from others. Make a list of your accomplishments or the challenges you've overcome, then look at it while reminding yourself why you were hired. Read through your résumé if you need to. Or you can use the same technique that helps you deal with the blow to your ego that you'll likely encounter if you've been laid off: Find someone you trust, let them go on about how good you are, and really listen.

Are you new to a job or a project and your lack of familiarity is causing your doubt? This is very common with new responsibilities. Around four to six weeks into them, we tend to wonder whether we're in over our heads. In that case, besides reinforcement, simply push through. The more often you do it, the easier it gets. If it's situationally specific, such as a tough meeting, an elegantly simple approach from Katy Milkman is to clap your hands together and say, "I'm excited to do this!" I've used it multiple times and vouch for its effectiveness.

There are times when you might need to tap dance, and if you do, keep this in mind: Most people aren't thinking about you all the time; they're thinking about themselves. In one example, I had just taken over a mutual fund investment area and was introduced as the new expert in investments. Keep in mind that investments is a highly technical field with its own elaborate jargon, and I had to look up some pretty standard terminology shortly before the meeting. In another, I was introduced as the head of our product team that had multiple reinsurance arrangements worth billions of dollars, and one of our top reinsurers wanted to meet with us. Again, I had been Googling some of the basic types and terms of reinsurance right before the meeting.

In both cases, it was helpful to remember that these folks who were visiting were trying to sell to me. They were eager to come in and talk about why *they* were good and how much *they* knew. They weren't trying to test *my* knowledge but wanted to show me *theirs*. So for both meetings, after some initial introductions I said something like, "You know, we get a lot of different opinions as to what's going on in the market right now. What do *you* think is most important? Where do *you* see things going? What's working for *you*?"

In both cases, they spent most of the meetings answering those questions and later walked out smiling.

> *If you encounter imposter syndrome, reinforce yourself and rely on the human nature of others to focus on themselves.*

Walking to Stockholm

Adversity is inevitable. Don't be surprised by it, and don't let it shut you down. I had a friend of mine, an excellent long-distance runner, who described his philosophy like this: "I see a hill, and I get ready to take it. I know there's downhill on the other side."

Embrace a challenge when you run into it.

Another friend of mine was raised in Moscow. When he and his brother were in their late teens, his uncle came home with bad news about his parents, who were both university professors who'd spoken out against the government.

"They've been taken away."

"When will they be back?"

"I don't think they will. Pack right now, pack light, and get out of Russia."

He and his brother walked eleven hundred kilometers to Helsinki, where they applied for asylum. Finland didn't grant it, so they kept walking to Stockholm, Sweden, where they were granted asylum.

This is a man who knew cold.

I was walking with him one January day after karate practice at MIT, and as I clutched my jacket and bounced up and down to stay warm, I asked him why he didn't seem affected by low temperatures.

"My father taught me," he said, "that when it's cold and the wind blows, you open your coat and embrace it."

As an old saying goes, "Obstacles aren't in the road. Obstacles don't block the road. Obstacles *are* the road."

> ***When confronted with adversity,***
> ***embrace the opportunity.***

Summary

Challenges and adversity can make you stronger if you approach them as opportunities to learn and improve. Here's how:

- *Accept the opportunity, the silver lining, presented by challenges.*
- *Frame your challenges, break problems into chunks, and focus on what's critical and controllable.*
- *Reassess and take inventory of your strengths and assets after a setback.*
- *Build your strength a little at a time by taking on gradually harder challenges.*
- *Be persistent. Ask lots of questions about everything until it's all clear.*

- *When confronting a challenge, be aware of self-imposed limitations and maintain naive optimism.*
- *Once again, relationships matter.*
- *When in doubt, reinforce yourself, and remember that the other person doesn't know everything either.*
- *Embrace adversity.*

Chapter 9

Better Yet—Process Improvements and Turnarounds

Companies and organizations have long focused on improving processes. During World War II, the US Army turned it into a science called "operations research" to improve logistics at scale under conditions in which better processes literally save lives. In the 1950s, W. Edwards Deming honed those processes for the civilian world.

In corporations, process improvement is often touted as a way to improve quality, as in Deming's case, or to reduce costs. I believe continual process improvement, specifically as applied to solving problems for your customers, is the only sustainable path to long-term profitability. The bigger a problem we solve for them, the more we're allowed to make and the happier the customer is to pay to fix whatever issue they have.

In this chapter, we'll cover the following questions:

- *What are the first steps I should take when assessing how a process can be improved?*
- *How much process improvement is enough?*
- *What measures help improve processes, and how should I apply them?*

- *How does segregating variation help improve processes?*
- *How do humans fit into the equation?*
- *Why focus on bottlenecks?*
- *When is it time to set a tough target?*

Take a Closer Look

If you want to make a system better, you first need to understand how it currently works (or more often, how it doesn't). Taking over a new area, or have a systemic problem that seems to keep coming back? Get immersed in the business at ground level and end to end.

You need direct visual observation to make this happen, and by that I mean sitting or standing with people and watching them work. Don't *describe* what they do, *watch* what they do. Even if you're a senior or mid-level leader, I encourage some periodic direct observation to maximize what you learn. However, I have a few caveats.

Having somebody at a senior level sit with you can be intimidating. To ease minds, assure folks that you're there to watch and learn from someone who knows their stuff and does it every day. You're not there to suggest changes. That would be micromanagement, and you haven't seen the whole process yet to be able to fix anything anyway. You're there to understand.

Another way I've made observations more comfortable is by not allowing the person's immediate boss to be there. Because this makes them more relaxed, individuals tend to open up more, avoid sugar-coating issues, and be more authentic. You get input that's unfiltered.

I've found in most cases that people appreciate the attention of a senior manager who's trying to understand their frustrations, and they enjoy being asked questions about what they do, as long as you're genuine and interested.

> ***Observe directly.***

The Enemy of the Good

According to archaeological records, sharks have been around for about 450 million years while humans or human-like beings only somewhere between two and six million. If sharks are such perfect killing machines that they've been around over one hundred times longer than us, why are we even here?

One explanation is to reinterpret the shorthand for Darwin's theory of evolution from "survival of the fittest" to "non-survival of the not fit enough." In other words, an animal doesn't need to be perfect to survive, it just needs to be better than those it's competing with. It needs to be good *enough*. It's the same with process fixes. If you spend too much time looking for the perfect answer, you never get time to implement anything. You need to make some decisions and move forward.

In addition to delays, there are other problems in looking for a perfect answer. In the real world, you often don't have perfect information. Ten people may have twenty different descriptions of a process. Processes are dynamic, and volume flow through a process changes along with the knowledge of the people working it, making processes rife with inconsistencies. There are also competing priorities. While you're trying to squeeze out the last 1 percent improvement on a $10 million a year process, there's a competing process that's 100 percent broken and costing $20 million a year in damage.

In 1897, economist Vilfredo Pareto espoused his famous 80/20 rule, stemming from a study of land ownership in England where 20 percent of landowners held 80 percent of the land. In a broader context, the concept is that 80 percent of outcomes are the result of 20 percent of causes. In real life with process improvement, I've seen this rule show up many times, and sometimes to an even greater extent. In the small-plan retirement business, for example, 5 percent of our brokers sold 95 percent of the business. We focused on them and grew sales by 50 percent.

Why is the 80/20 rule important? It lets you know where to focus. In the old days, for example, retirement plan providers sent quarterly statements to customers. At one company, we went through a multimillion-dollar technology upgrade to improve the statements, only to find after many delays stemming from a desire to be perfect that customers didn't like the changes. Going back to the drawing board and directly observing customers read and react to sample statements in different formats, we found that the first thing they looked for was their account balance. So, we ditched all the detailed work we'd done and replaced it with a re-redesigned statement that showed their balance at the top of the first page in extra-large font and outlined in a box. Simple, cheaper, and customers loved it!

Here's a shortcut in the similar spirit of focusing on what's most important: In almost every one of over fifty improvement efforts I've been a part of, the people doing the actual work requested better information about how things stood during processing. And these updates are more important in insurance and financial services than in a social setting. Instead of "Where's my pizza?" people are asking things like "Have I been approved?" and "Did you get my check?" and "Does Mom have a place to live?"

Just go ahead and make readily available status updates part of the solution for your next process improvement effort. If you go through exhaustive analysis, it will show up as something you need to do anyway.

> ***Don't seek perfection. Fix the big stuff and move on.***

How Am I Doing So Far?

That last recommendation, providing an update as to how things are going, is a form of measurement. You need to measure your outcomes to see whether you've made progress. Start with one critical requirement though. Measure what's important to and has the most impact on the customer.

Watch out here! I've seen multiple situations where the effort at improvement presupposes the answer and the team doing the process improvement work fools themselves. In the early days of the internet, for instance, one team fought hard for and justified a budget spend by saying "Customers want to interact with us electronically." They never observed a customer to see whether that was true, but they knew that an electronic data request was a lot cheaper than a telephone call with a trained and licensed rep and would result in budget savings. When we put in the new tools for people to get data electronically, call center volume went up, not down, proving that when it comes to life-critical decisions, people want the comfort of a human, even if all the person on the other end of the line does is confirm what they were going to do anyway.

Process measurements can also be simple. In Maine, we initially managed a multibillion-dollar line of business with two pieces of legal paper, one for the assets we bought and one for the deals we struck with large customers. It wasn't perfect, but it told us whether we were in the ballpark. When we later automated it and made it electronic, it didn't really lead to vastly different decisions.

Measuring also has the benefit of increasing visibility. When you administer a retirement plan, you periodically receive money and a list of who it belongs to. At one point with one company, we had multiple ways of accepting deposits (check, wire, bank debit) from a retirement plan, with a listing of whose it was (paper, diskette, fax, email, electronic). We began a campaign for getting customers to convert to a common electronic tool that would improve quality, reduce the workload of the customer, and reduce costs from twenty dollars per transaction to six cents. Despite a compelling proposition, take-up rate was slow. Our initial measurement attempt, a fancy set of consultant-provided barcode scanners to track time, failed to produce insights or results. But an operations manager achieved quick results using a whiteboard and an erasable magic marker. The first week I toured his area, the board had about fifteen names on it along with the number of conversions each person had completed. Most were around ten, one outlier at the low end was at two, and one at the high end was at twenty. Without a change in process but merely by posting the results, by the time I visited the team the following week the tens were all twenties, the twenty was over forty, and the one at two had left the company. After one week.

One mentor often reminded me that "You manage what you measure," meaning you can change an outcome simply by picking the right metric. For example, it was common that a sales team would figure out the new year's compensation plan on the first day it was published and take advantage of any loopholes. By contrast, when working with the head of sales we once put in a sales plan in January to measure "weighted sales." It gave more credit for more profitable business and less credit for less profitable business. The result was almost immediate. By March, profitable sales were up 30 percent and unprofitable sales down 30 percent. Both were a core part of improving profits by a factor of six.

One final example of the power of visual and physical examples is when Adam, our Six Sigma Master Black Belt (a special process improvement designation requiring years of training), had just completed a project with his team to reduce the number of pages in quarterly statements mailed to customers. He came into a glass-walled conference room that had all the blinds down for privacy, showed a box and a half full of statements, and said, "These are the statements we sent this quarter to customers."

A few executives stifled yawns.

"Here's what it used to look like." With that and a sweep of his hand, Adam raised the blinds to reveal his team standing outside with crates and crates of overflowing paper. One single customer had received a box every month just for their own statements.

No more yawns, and a round of applause commenced.

> *Use measurement to track process improvement. Pick your measures carefully and make them visual when possible.*

Escaping a Bind

One of the challenges with processes can be achieving consistency. The more complicated and customized a process is, the harder it is to replicate with quality. I had an assistant who often quoted her dad regarding an old compound technology: "Never buy a TV/VCR combination. If either part breaks, then the whole thing breaks."

Larger customers especially prefer a great deal of customization. Yet the vast number of customers don't need what those big customers do, nor do they have the resources to pay for it, much less evaluate it. This dichotomy can cause problems, and I stumbled across a metaphor many years ago that has helped make it clear: Suppose you have a perfectly spherical basketball. If you have a reasonable level of skill (more than I have), it shouldn't be that challenging to dribble it well and under control. Now suppose you get a little bump on that basketball, a variation from the perfect sphere. Most of the time you can still dribble well and under control, but every once in a while you hit that bump and don't know where the ball will go. Now imagine that same ball with three or four bumps on it. That's all you need to make it wildly uncontrollable. Add a small amount of variation to a process, such as exceptions for each of three or four large customers, and like those few bumps on a basketball the whole thing breaks down.

It's a more common challenge than you think, and here's a caution for you: It's not uncommon to have one of your expense experts do a cost study and declare that a variation, a little bump, is small and will cost you only, say, $1,000 a month for the extra time it takes to make the exception. That's wrong, and it misses the big picture. The problem is not the added cost of the extra step for the single large customer but the change in or interruption to your standard process for thousands or even millions of other customers. In other words, it's the whole basketball. In my experience, that cost can be up to one hundred times the base-calculated cost. And even worse, variations compound.

So with stakes that large, how do you manage variation when you have so many requests for it? One way is to segregate variation. An example that's proved effective occurred when I worked with three different process improvement experts who all had worked with the same prior employer. Each gave a slightly different perspective on a story about their office supply company's attempted upgrade. One of the company's product lines was three-ring binders. In an effort to reduce costs, they purchased a pair of big, new, and expensive top-of-the-line machines to manufacture the binders. They eagerly looked at their manufacturing costs (measure!) and found that (Oh no!) they had gone up, not down as expected given the substantial investment.

With analysis, they found the culprit. They had ten thousand different SKUs, or types of binders of different sizes, materials, and widths. Every time they switched over the machines for a new SKU, it took time to remove the old material, insert the new, and program the instructions for the next batch of binders.

They developed a simple, but excellent solution. They used the new machines for the top two hundred highest-volume SKUs and for the other 9,800 brought out some of the old machines, or even in some cases of low run sizes, produced the materials manually. They went one step further. A separate area was set up to go back to a couple thousand smaller customers each year and offer them a choice: "We no longer offer the model you last purchased. However, if you choose one of these other options, we can save you some money." If the customer chose not to buy, then the company stopped producing that version.

This approach had multiple benefits. The new machine ran at high volumes per run with a lot less time spent switching over, the volume of high-run SKUs increased, and the variation went down even on the old business. Customers saved money, quality went up, and their unit costs went down dramatically.

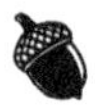 *Segregate and drive out variation to improve quality and reduce costs.* 

Feeling Pinched

Eliyahu M. Goldratt's *The Goal* introduces valuable concepts presented as a novel for accessibility. Though its cultural context feels dated, akin to the show *Mad Men*, a key concept is identifying bottlenecks, steps in the process that not only leave somebody lined up and waiting to go through that step but also prevent a whole bunch of people downstream from that process from performing their own steps while they wait for output.

A common solution is adding alternate resources to relieve the bottleneck, as seen in the three-ring binder example in which older machines handled small-batch variations. While not the only approach, this strategy often effectively increases throughput at critical stages. In one company's 401(k) business, for example, I had an underwriter who was excellent and could handle the most complex cases, but he always had a long backlog of cases waiting to go through his process. This caused him a lot of distress, and he was constantly in a foul mood, snapping at people with whom he'd had a great relationship for a long time.

To clear out the bottleneck, we used a combination of segregation of variability and additional resources. We brought in some junior resources for the simplest cases and left our grizzled veteran to handle the more complex ones. I told him he was the mechanic in the backroom to whom we'd go when no one else could fix the engine.

We also freed up some of his time by taking some simpler work off his plate, which was a key component. Both steps removed the bottleneck and dramatically improved speed and throughput. The underwriter ended up so happy that he sometimes sang at his desk.

Technology can be a big help with removing bottlenecks, but it must be used correctly, keeping in mind the 80/20 rule. In the underwriting case, besides making our veteran underwriter more effective, we applied a simple technology fix to make the rest of the team more effective too. One of the most frustrating steps for our salespeople was waiting for the underwriting on run-of-the-mill quotes, so a summer intern programmed a quote tool for these simplest cases, building it in a protected Excel spreadsheet that we sent out on disks. Our IT area went nuts: "You have to go through protocols and testing before you release a new capability!" They changed their minds when they found out that the solution reduced turnaround time for quotes from six weeks to six minutes.

We did, admittedly, have a few bugs, but because the code was written in a simple system, we just revised it and sent new disks. Once the bugs were removed and the process was improved, we mainstreamed the solution into our established systems. That approach, testing a system in plaster before casting it in bronze, became not only acceptable to IT but our standard of practice for new efforts going forward.

There are other key considerations with bottlenecks as well. For one thing, they work their way through a system from one location to another just like a sheep works its way through a python that's devouring it. Deal with the bottleneck that's causing the most pain first, which is often but not always the one that's highest upstream in the process, and keep in mind that in determining "causing the most pain," you're looking for the highest direct or indirect impact on the customer—their pain, not yours.

Next, when you free up one bottleneck, especially if it's far upstream, you create more work downstream and often a new bottleneck. In the underwriting example, because the quote process became faster, sales went up and we had to process onboarding of new clients at higher volumes. It's a sign that your process improvement is working, but be ready for it, and plan ahead if you can.

> ***Remove bottlenecks and, as you do,***
> ***watch for subsequent effects.***

Stretch!

Sometimes what a team needs most is clarity.

The leader of a group can provide this, if needed, with an edict setting a tough target. The target should not be the answer, the *how* of the fix. The target should be the *objective*, leaving the particular approach up to the team, and it will benefit from feeling a bit ridiculous, almost but not quite unattainable. An order of magnitude change will wake someone up and get them to rethink a process, while an incrementally higher target won't.

"We want to cut the average number of pages in a statement from fourteen to two."

"I want processing to be end-to-end electronic, with no manual intervention required, not even once."

"We need real-time quotes, not quotes six weeks later."

When a senior leader once took over a new area and mandated that the number of monthly reports be cut in half, an *almost* impossible target, one team blanched.

The key word is "almost." The team started cutting out three or four reports a month, along with sending a note: "We're no longer producing this report. If it causes any problems, please let me know." Very few complaints followed, and the number of reports dropped not by half but from forty-one to four!

There was also a side benefit. The teams producing the reports had spent tons of time reconciling them with each other, but because they no longer had to, they saved time for more meaningful work and the values were more reliable.

> ***When a team needs a nudge, set a high but achievable target.***

Stepping Out of Line

In college, my civil engineer roommate came back from class one day excited about what he'd learned. This enthusiasm was out of his daily character in a high-pressure engineering school, so I asked him to explain.

In the old days of building projects, he said, efficiency was the name of the game. You tried to do all similar activities at the same time. You framed all the buildings at once, poured concrete all at once, and landscaped all at once. But when project engineers designing college campuses sought that efficiency by pouring all the sidewalks at the same time and planting the grass right afterward, they ran into a problem: Students walked on the new grass instead of the sidewalks.

In response, the engineers put up signs that read, "Please do not walk on the grass." Students did anyway. Engineers then put up fences to protect the grass, but students seeking the shortest route to or from class tore them down or jumped over them and still walked on the grass.

Finally, the engineers changed their approach. They didn't put in sidewalks the first year, instead observing where the students walked. They then put the sidewalks there and planted grass around them, no signs necessary. The students walked on the sidewalks, and the grass grew in lush and green.

> ***Assess the users of the process you're improving,***
> ***and tailor your response to them.***

Summary

Improving processes is its own specialized discipline, and it can be enhanced by applying specific techniques either singly or in combination:

- *Observe directly. Go to the source to understand.*
- *Don't try to be perfect. Fix the big stuff first, reach "good enough," and move on.*
- *Measure the most important components of your processes, and make measurement as accessible, concrete, and tangible as possible.*
- *Segregate variation!*

- *Identify and remove bottlenecks and consider the down-stream consequences.*
- *When you need to, lead from the top by setting a tough target.*
- *Keep your improvements intuitive and reflective of the needs of those who use the process you're fixing.*

Chapter 10

Mostly Carrots—Managing and Motivating Individuals and Teams

Being able to motivate a person or a group is critical because knowing what to do is one thing, but doing it is another, and in order to get something done we need people to do it.

Keeping teams aligned and motivated is critical to success. The higher we rise in an organization, the more people are looking at us for their sense of drive and purpose. Even at a lower level, our employees, colleagues, and even sometimes our more senior leaders will gain their enthusiasm from ours.

In this chapter, we'll cover the following questions:

- *How do I let my team know I care?*
- *How do I tailor my interactions with the team?*
- *How important is visibility, and how do I provide it?*
- *What's the best way to provide praise so that it's motivating?*
- *How do I leverage explicit and implicit team autonomy?*
- *In what situations should I take authority back?*
- *In what ways can I establish expectations that motivate?*

- *How does accountability relate to motivation?*
- *How do I motivate people who don't report to me?*
- *How do I motivate myself during big changes?*
- *How do I deal with the impact of negative employees on motivation?*
- *How can measuring skills development help with motivation?*

Be Involved, and Be Seen

To be motivated, people, especially your employees, need to know you care.

One way to demonstrate you care is to get to know them. Just as with assessing a problem or process, you can't get the most out of a team unless you know them. You need to immerse yourself.

As I mentioned early on, when I took over a team of eighty actuaries, students, and support staff, I met for half an hour to forty-five minutes with each person individually to get to know them, their background, what they were working on, and what their expected career path was. That put me in a better position to make decisions about what the team should take on and what strengths and weaknesses we had in total. It also showed interest in what development to pursue and what opportunities to provide. Critically, it got each employee thinking about their own roles and responsibilities for their careers and what motivated them.

Another approach to demonstrate connection is to make yourself visible, and side-by-side visibility means more than seeing you on a stage or a remote group meeting screen. If there's a team working overtime at 7:00 at night, you'd better show up at 7:00 at night and talk with them. You can't ask them to do anything you wouldn't do yourself. When I took over an investment team that was having trouble and working late hours, I brought them brownies, pretzels, and water, not because they needed a snack but because they needed to know someone was aware of their situation and wanted to improve it. Then I sat with them while they worked through a backlog, not because I could help or offer advice but, again, so that they were aware of my commitment to them.

Similarly, when one of my teams went through Lean Six Sigma training, I'd been through it before, gotten a "green belt" in process management, and already worked through a few dozen process improvement efforts. I didn't need the training and didn't expect to get any new information out of attending the class, yet I went through the same training as everyone else anyway. They saw me there failing and succeeding with them, committed to development and growth. And I picked up a few new things I'd missed before.

 *Immerse yourself to get to know your team, and make yourself visible to them.* 

Fit to Suit

Once you know your team, tailor your interactions to them. Every person and every team is different.

My investment team had widely differing backgrounds and objectives. I worked with quant jock investment experts who thought they knew more than everyone else because they had such a technical focus, sales teams where ego was critical, and operations folks who were kind of like a goalie. In fact, my treasurer once said, "If I do my job well, nobody notices. If I do it poorly, everyone does." When I talked with the quant jocks it revolved around technical issues, with the sales team it was about what they needed to complete a deal or improve a relationship, and with operations managers it was about the problems they were trying to fix. The key was not to suppress their individual identities but to celebrate them, to let them be good at what they were good at and proud of it.

When we started a new line of business helping primarily doctors and dentists reduce their debt costs by refinancing student loans, we had to start the team off on the right foot. After first demonstrating the behavior myself, I asked them to share with everyone else on the team one of their strengths and one behavior we should watch out for and call each other on if we started to exhibit it. That gave power to the team, as well as the right to disagree and, importantly, a way to do it.

Often, a single person will adopt a contrary position, even without being designated. Let them. If there's no one in that contrary position, you may have to take it yourself, even if you appear contradictory. One way is simply to ask, "What if we're wrong about that?" It's good to listen to your disruptors, but insist that they disagree with respect, and leave time for others.

Keep in mind that too strong a consensus can indicate that each team member is thinking alike, but it can also mean that your team is afraid of opposing you and of speaking up. To resolve this issue in one group, we designated someone each week to play devil's advocate: "Whatever the rest of the team says, your job is to argue with it, for today, until we reach a decision." It worked so well that after half a dozen meetings, we didn't need the designated position anymore. People were speaking their minds.

> ***Adjust your interactions with individuals and teams to be relevant to them and what they care about most.***

You Did It!

How to Talk So Kids Will Listen & Listen So Kids Will Talk by Adele Faber and Elaine Mazlish has excellent advice on how to give praise. Although it's geared toward parent–child relationships, it works remarkably well for motivating adults. The main idea is to be specific, describe what you see, and let the child (person) praise themself.

Imagine commending your child who's coloring in a picture book with "Nice job!" It's praise, but it doesn't tell the child what they did well, and the natural inclination of the child (or an employee) is to question the source. *Is it really good, or is he just saying that because he's my dad* (or she because she's my boss)?

Here's an alternative if you want your child to learn to color inside the lines: "Wow! You really stayed within the lines on that one." You've only expressed an observation, not an opinion as to quality. But your child is likely to immediately infer that coloring inside the lines is good. The praise comes from within, so the next time they try to stay inside the lines.

This can also work in reverse. Suppose you want to raise an independent and creative child who doesn't stay inside the lines. Just change the observation: "Wow! You used four different colors!" or "Wow! You colored every part on the page that your mind took you to."

At work, it might be one of these:

- "I noticed you spoke up and defended yourself in that meeting."
- "You made a hard decision there."
- "You really thought that through."
- "That's the clearest summary I've ever heard of a complex set of issues."

Keep your praise legitimate or it won't be believable, but look for opportunities to provide it, ideally right after you've seen the praiseworthy behavior. One author says we need about four and a half positive comments to offset one negative one.

Keep in mind that simply showing respect by listening to someone is an implicit form of praise. It says, "I admire your view enough to put value on it." Everyone wants recognition that their contributions are beneficial and that their thoughts are valid.

 **_Praise with objective observation to elicit the behavior you'd like to see repeated._** 

Agency and Urgency

People have to be part of the solution, and that doesn't mean just telling them over and over what the answer is. They have to be part of both coming up with it and implementing it.

A memorable psychology experiment conducted in 1971 demonstrates just how much we value our sense of control.[1] Subjects were split into two groups, and each was measured on their performance of a routine task while a loud, distracting noise played nearby. All experiment elements were the same for the two groups except one: Group A were told if they wanted to stop the loud noise, all they had to do was press a button. Group B had no button. Not surprisingly, Group A performed much better on their task. Surprisingly,

---

1. David C. Glass, Bruce Reim, and Jerome E. Singer, "Behavioral Consequences of Adaptation to Controllable and Uncontrollable Noise," *Journal of Experimental Social Psychology* 7, no. 2 (1971): 244–257, https://doi.org/10.1016/0022-1031(71)90070-9.

however, most of the people in Group A did not elect to press the button. The sense of control, the *option* to get rid of the noise, is what helped them perform better, not actually doing anything about the distraction.

This experiment supports the idea that if you provide your team with the autonomy to take action, even on small things, they maintain a sense of control and are more motivated. In chapter 11, I give some fun examples with autonomy over a wastebasket and photocopier.

The approach of imbuing confidence and expectation by providing agency works as well in the real world as it does in a psychology experiment. When I came back to work after being out for several weeks after my wife died, one of the first things the team put in front of me was a two-option choice for how to handle an old block of underperforming business. They had been through hours of intense discussions with each other and wanted to know which option I preferred so that I could break the tie and we could move ahead. Timing was overdue, and we were already at the last second on some deadlines.

Despite the time crunch, I asked them to go back as a team and return with a recommendation rather than a choice. They were senior leaders and in charge. They didn't need me making their decisions for them. They had a recommendation for me the next day. Better still, their ongoing behavior changed rapidly after that, and I'd come into meetings being told what the team had decided rather than being asked for my decision.

 **Give your teams agency, autonomy, and a sense of control.** 

A Stake in the Ground

Although delegated authority is the ideal, just as with facing challenges and when problem-solving in general, there are times when a team gets stuck and you need to lead. If you've tried pushing back and asking your team for a recommendation and they're still stuck, try again.

There are times, though, when you've debated an issue long enough that you have to make a call. When to do that is a matter of judgment, but one sign is that you've heard the same arguments again and again. For example, under prior leadership, one team had been discussing for over four years an outsourcing effort that would cost more than $150 million. In an effort to create agency, I let the debate continue a while longer, and there were strong, viable arguments on both sides. It was clear after that additional debate, though, that we weren't going to reach consensus, so I made a decision.

There wasn't really a big downside in either direction (otherwise the decision would've been easier), except one: A decision to move ahead was declarative; we were taking action. If I'd said, even definitively, that we were not going to outsource, it still would've left the debate open. So, I let the team know that I'd heard and considered all their arguments and that we were going ahead. Even the opponents of that option were relieved.

Sometimes a team just needs action for the sense of progress. If two choices are roughly comparable, choose the one that provides that sense of progress.

> *When warranted, and after trying to let a team decide on their own, make a decision.*

Call AAA

Another motivational tool for teams is to establish a set of principles.

One example of something that at first appeared hokey but really worked comes from when I worked in a corporate environment with one of the most distributed decision-making frameworks I've ever seen. No one wanted to make a decision without everyone weighing in and agreeing. Within that stultifying atmosphere, our group of actuaries was replete with really smart people, but I thought we were challenged at both communicating what we worked on and driving decisions without asking for permission too often. I set out a very simple mnemonic device, which I've been able to use elsewhere, even in organizations with better decision-making contexts. It was AAA: Analyze. Advocate. Act.

Our team was great at the analysis part, but I wanted them to take a position because you get more commitment that way. In figuring out how to develop that sense of commitment, I thought back to when our kids were young and my wife and I went to a kindergarten parent night to find out what one of them would be learning. The teacher gave a demonstration of how they involve kids with learning, using three beakers of colored water placed at the front of the classroom in which we were meeting, one filled with red, one with blue, and the other with yellow. The example she provided was to ask the kids what would happen if she mixed the red and yellow water together.

"It'll turn pink," says Jamie, stating her favorite color.

"Everyone who thinks it'll be pink line up behind Jamie."

"It will turn brown," says Billy. Those who agree line up behind him.

"Orange," says Marcus, and he gets a few believers in his line.

Now, how eager are these kids to see what happens when you mix the beakers together?

I advised my actuaries something similar. Before they ran a model, I asked them to guess at the results. "Why?" they asked. "That's why I built the model." I explained it was so that they were committed to the answer and looking for the connections between cause and effect.

So again, the Analyze part was good.

Advocate means to argue as to why your answer is preferred, to take a side, to get a debate going, then commit.

Even if you do both of those things, but nothing gets implemented, you've failed. So, the third step is to Act. I don't care if it's someone else's responsibility, just follow through and make sure the decision gets implemented. That not only gives a higher likelihood of execution but gets you talking with and learning about other areas.

> *Look for ways to connect with your team and commit them to the output of their work. A simple mnemonic can remind them of expectations and instill pride.*

Who's on First?

It's one thing to motivate a team of people who work directly for you. It's even harder to work with people across an organization. Though many of the same principles apply as for your own team, I have one additional recommendation: Establish accountability through point people.

I worked at one time with multiple lawyers because each had their own special discipline. Tax law is very different from insurance law, the DOL's rules for retirement plans, the SEC's rules for investments, antitrust rules, and contract law. Additionally, each lawyer had their own personality, opinions, biases, and language. I moved to one point person for the law department, telling them, "You are my main contact. You go back to the legal team, run shuttle negotiation and translation across law, and let me know the one consolidated opinion of the department. I will only take counsel that drives a decision from *you*, no one else." The point person had one other job, which was to translate and communicate any decisions to all the impacted lawyers.

Similarly, with a sales team that wasn't under my direct control, I got multiple requests a day for different exceptions, product ideas, or marketing changes. I finally agreed with the head of sales that although I was glad to listen to all the ideas, when it came to prioritizing what we'd work on, I was listening to only a single person he delegated to. The approach worked like a charm in both places, so I extended it to IT, operations, marketing, and other areas.

When you work across lines, it's hard to share relevant information because you don't know what the other area you're dealing with needs, and they don't know what you need. My team and I once had a very successful knowledge exchange with an area that was automating the use of robots (before AI). Bots in insurance would essentially replicate the more mundane tasks that worked across systems. Each had its own employee ID number and might log in (per your instructions), extract data, put it into another system, perform a calculation, and share it with a third system. We sat with this automation team and simply walked through the top five or ten business problems we were trying to solve, then they walked through five or ten robotic applications they'd developed in other areas. We shared both successes and mistakes, and we prioritized the top three things we'd work on together.

There's one last rule of thumb I've used to great success to decide when to involve a lot of people and when to stick to a small number and maintain accountability: Information-sharing should be broad, while decision-making should be narrow.

> ***Designate single points of contact to both establish clear accountability and ease decision-making.***

Substitute

One particular demotivator for many people is a big change in an organization. Change is hard. Big change, such as a shift in the strategic direction of a company, a divisional reorganization, or new leadership, is harder.

One of the reasons change is hard is the sense of loss that accompanies it. In the same spirit of trading up versus giving up, which we talked about in chapter 7, one way to keep an organization motivated during times of change is to set a new target. It's a lot easier to stop focusing on the old way you used to do it once you have a new target to shoot for. Even with all the other aspects of change management, give somebody that new target, even if metaphoric, early on in the process.

On a personal level, one situation during which you might run into change is after you've switched jobs. Typically, four to six weeks into a new role you become discouraged. There's a whole new lexicon to pick up, you need to learn who the doers versus the talkers are, and you usually have a new culture to adapt to. To motivate yourself at a time like this, remind yourself of your new objectives, whether they're what you're trying to do at work or your personal objectives around growth and learning. That will help you push through.

> **Motivate during times of change by establishing new objectives.**

Addition Through Subtraction

One counterintuitive motivator is getting rid of a toxic employee.

I don't mean layoffs. If you do a good job at prioritization and communication, you ought to be able to avoid or at least dampen the need for large layoffs.

I also don't mean letting someone go because they're different. Diversity of opinion and approach can dramatically enhance the performance of a group when well-executed. You don't want to be hiring people just because they're like you. In fact, if you're good like Abe Lincoln, you hire people who complement you.

There are times, though, when one employee can bring the whole group down, whether through their poor performance that requires the rest of the team to pick up their slack or through a pervasively negative attitude or behavior. On the few occasions when I let that person go, there was a collective sigh of relief from everyone who remained, and results dramatically improved.

> **Watch out for and eliminate toxic behavior to help keep a team motivated.**

From Doughnuts to Hex Nuts

About the time my uncle Phil reached age seventy, I asked him how he was doing. He'd retired a few years earlier after several decades working with a company that made flour and a few related items, including doughnuts.

"Fantastic! I just started a new job," he told me.

"Really? What's so good about it?"

"It's for a regional hardware store, kind of like a Home Depot or Lowe's but on a smaller scale."

I knew he had a penchant for fixing things up, so this seemed right up his alley. "Tell me more."

"Well, I started at minimum wage."

That didn't sound too appealing to me.

"Then, every time I show I've learned something new I get a raise."

"Something new? Like what?"

"I've done Paint I and Paint II, All About Grass, and Small Engine Repair."

This was getting interesting.

"Every time I show I know my stuff, they pay me more."

"How do you show what you know?"

"There's a test. They quiz me. Then I have to give a class explaining it to someone else."

He had more energy and enthusiasm about his job than a new puppy does when playing, and more pride in it than someone who's just been the first in their family to graduate from college.

In the 1950s, my dad described a similar approach used in the US Army, which he narrates with similar pride. He was in the motor pool and needed to learn to repair large wheeled vehicles. Each week, the class learned about a system, such as cooling (radiator), tires, or exhaust, and at the end of the week they faced a vehicle with a problem in that system and tried to diagnose and fix it. If someone succeeded, they moved on to the next system, but if someone failed to figure it out or repair it, they repeated the process until they got it right (or were assigned somewhere else). As a final exam, aspiring mechanics faced a vehicle with multiple issues and didn't know which systems were affected. This time those who were successful graduated, and the top two soldiers were to be given a choice of duty across Europe.

My dad came in second, then found that they'd cut back the prize to one person only. However, he was able to select a job on base and ended up with a much bigger reward. As he was driving the mail truck around base, he met a young Missouri girl at one stop, liked her, and asked her what she most missed about the States.

"Women's magazines," came the reply.

The next week, he delivered a stack of them to her desk.

Shortly after returning stateside, they married, and a few years after that, I was born.

I contrast the excitement and pride of both brothers with the typical performance review process at work. While my dad and uncle were both eager and inspired to get feedback and to learn, periodic work reviews tend to be demotivating, even for top performers, and they're full of traps for managers. They sometimes get misused and abused and are often a source of frustration for everyone involved.

That's not to say that there's no value in consistent, regularly scheduled feedback. There is! It's easy to let slip a conversation about how things are going or what you need from someone next. More than once, I thought I did an excellent job apprising someone on their progress but later found out that I hadn't. Process helps.

However, the focus of those scheduled discussions ought to be on skills development, whether hard skills (the nuts and bolts of doing your job, like my uncle) or soft skills (such as how you get along with other people, like my dad, who became a guidance counselor). Shifting that focus has completely changed the motivational aspects of performance discussions.

Whether it's learning to repair small engines, fix trucks, fold a band saw, or read a spreadsheet, we like to acquire new skills because it provides a sense of progress.

***Focus performance discussions
on skills development.***

Summary

Knowledge is often factual, but knowledge alone isn't enough. You need people to get things done. Keeping a team aligned and motivated is critical to success. Remember these techniques:

- *Immerse yourself, get to know people as well as processes, and be visible.*
- *Tailor your interactions based on what drives individuals and teams the most.*
- *Praise with description rather than evaluation.*

- *Impart true authority and trust, both explicitly and implicitly, by your actions.*
- *Delegated authority is the goal, but sometimes you have to lead from the front.*
- *Connect teams to their outputs.*
- *Use designated accountable point people.*
- *If you want to motivate people who don't report to you (or who do!), keep in mind what's in it for them.*
- *To ease change, replace outdated targets with new ones.*
- *Get rid of toxic employees who drag down a team.*
- *Track skills progress to motivate people.*

Chapter 11

Bringing Business, People, and Processes Together

Thinkers as different as military strategist Carl von Clausewitz, scientist and philosopher Albert Einstein, and boxer Mike Tyson all espouse the same advice, just in different language. Theory is great, but that doesn't mean it will work in practice.

We've covered a lot in this section, including communication, decision-making and prioritization, adversity, process improvements, and motivation. In this chapter, we'll examine real-life applications of these concepts during multifaceted struggles representative of those that many leaders encounter. Let's see how they work, and don't, in the real world. Some strategies failed and some ultimately succeeded, but all resulted in lessons that my team and I learned throughout the process.

Florida Man Returns

In the introduction, I described a challenging scenario heading up a defined benefit pension administration business in Florida, with three major obstacles:

1. No experience in an operations function

2. Multiple people problems, including skepticism and lack of engagement

3. A significant business problem of having an eighteen-month backlog coupled with negative earnings

Greek Menu

I first tried to solve the problem the same way I did early in my career: playing detective, asking lots of questions, and sitting with each of my team one-on-one, but nothing really budged.

At one point, I brought in half a dozen Six Sigma Black Belts, experts in process redesign using methods popularized by Deming in Japan with companies including Toyota before being repatriated to the US. They ran multiple all-day sessions with no progress. Why couldn't a whole panel of experts solve the problem? To this day I'm not absolutely sure, but I ascribe it mostly to two things. First, we tried to fix it in a conference room on a whiteboard. Second, we were looking for one big fix that would solve everything at once. Both made it too complicated.

What finally worked was a series of smaller, simpler steps with an underlying theme of real-world application. You'll notice several of the concepts we've reviewed when they're let out of their cages and face actual problems in the wild.

1. Visibility

I spent a lot of time walking the floor, being there at night if people were working overtime and checking in on them. "What's working?" I'd ask. "What are your biggest issues?" "Who are you waiting for most often before you can do your work?" "Who do you wish we had more of?" Rather than just complaining, folks started to open up more and bring problems and suggestions to my team and to me.

2. Real-Time Immersion

I watched people work, sitting at their desks with them and observing what they did. I didn't tell them what to do differently, I just asked questions. The only rule was that "Your boss can't be here to hear what you say." It made their bosses nuts, but it got me real-time information. I watched one woman work through a complicated and ingenious system of multicolored paper clips and sticky notes on two computers. She'd log into one for information, write it on the correct note based on the type of information it was, log out and into another computer to retrieve something there, then clip it to the appropriate file. It worked, but ouch. When I started figuring things out, I directed some of my team to go through the same process I had. After sitting with the same woman, my head of IT spent the weekend programming a fix that reduced the worker's two-foot-high pile of papers to a dozen sheets. She was then able to apply her really clever brain to more complex problems.

3. Find Bottlenecks

In previous organizations, I'd seen colleagues struggle with overly complex time allocation systems. In one, an IT leader was very proud that he could track every hour an employee spent. Another hired a consultant who had people scan bar codes when they started and stopped an effort. Both approaches had problems. First, knowing how much time you spent on something doesn't tell you why, or how you could make it better. Second, the total always added up to about 130 percent of the time available. Third, people hated it, maybe because the percentage of time allocated to figuring out how they spent their time was so high. Out of pure frustration, I landed on a simple solution during a senior staff meeting: "Bring me a list of the five busiest people in the organization." They did, and that gave us our priorities.

4. Quick, Simple Fixes

Reviewing the list of the busiest people, we found that one was Bob, an actuary with over forty years of experience who approved all the benefit calculations. As with the underwriting example I provided earlier, we were dependent on one person, an expert. It was a bottleneck, and we handled it in a similar way to the three-ring binder example. We broke benefit calcs into simple and complex, then gave the complex ones to Bob and the simple ones to junior folks who were up and coming, with Bob's guidance. Bob loved it because he was valued for his knowledge, wasn't wasting his time on simple stuff, and was training and mentoring people. His team loved it because they didn't have to go to him for approval on everything and then wait six weeks for it, and Bob's throughput went up about 500 percent (that's not an exaggeration). Then we dealt with the downstream impact. When we calculated benefits more quickly, the benefits processing team had a bigger stack of calculations to put into the system. When that team in turn eased their workload with a technology fix, the benefits payment team had much higher volume. In both cases, we applied the approach of providing additional less-skilled resources to ease the bottleneck.

5. Employee Engagement and Accountability

One of the most frustrating team members for my staff was one of our mid-manager operational leads. At corporate meetings, she had a reputation similar to a gadfly, always pointing out what was wrong and making my team crazy, to the point that a few of them avoided her. "She's always complaining," they'd say.

In her defense, she also always coupled a complaint with a proposed solution. That's why when I created a new employee engagement counsel, I put her in charge of it. Her job was two-fold: improve morale and prioritize which issues were the biggest aggravators for our employees. She was excellent at both, and her prioritization helped us focus on the right areas first. She was an integral component of identifying the bottleneck with Bob and resolving the downstream implications. By the time I left, she had set term limits on the employee council to handle the demand to be on it and had a waiting list of over twenty people wanting to participate.

If you want to instill change in an organization, you can't merely tell people what to do, even multiple times. You have to vest them in the process of fixing it. They need to participate.

Turned Around

With those changes, we eliminated the backlog, reduced the contractor load, and hung onto a few clients who'd been about to leave. The real measure of success for me, though, came during one of my nightly walkthroughs.

"What's with the palm trees?" I asked, spotting a picture on the cubicle wall.

"Well, for the first time in ten years, I'm going on vacation next week."

> *Prioritizing, being visible, immersing yourself, reducing bottlenecks, and encouraging employee engagement all work when applied correctly.*

The Other End of the Spectrum

The lessons I learned in Florida helped me manage other difficult situations better as well.

When I left Florida for a much closer job in Massachusetts, I faced what at first seemed like a completely different problem: starting up a new business in a category called "stable value." Almost all 401(k)-style retirement plans offer a menu of investment options to participating employees. One in most plans is a "safe" option, the only one you can choose that gives back a dollar plus interest for every dollar invested. You don't lose money, which is why it's called the stable value option.

When I arrived to build this new business, I ran into a number of challenges. First, I went from managing 180 people in Florida out of an office you could get lost in to managing a team of one, Paul, whom I directed from a dingy, tattered cubicle. Saved from a job elimination in another part of the company, Paul immediately became a kindred spirit. However, because of his background, he also knew nothing about stable value. With time and work, he became an expert.

I also managed to borrow a resource, Peggy, from another area. Working together, we discovered other challenges as well:

- There was no contract for customers to sign if we happened to write a deal.
- Our systems weren't set up to support this new line of business.
- We had no contacts we could market to and no salespeople who knew the space.
- The head of sales directed me that "We have real sales targets we need to hit this year. I don't need you distracting my salespeople with this new thing you're working on."

The approach to resolving these issues included many of the tools we've discussed.

Dogged Determination

I looked for something to connect the three of us to the mission, similar to the AAA mnemonic device I used with the actuaries years later, and I found a simple one. I posted a cartoon drawing of a massive bulldog, muscles bulging from under a spiked collar, holding a large bone like a weapon. Underneath it was written, "Like a dog with a bone, until our first stable value sale." We got to see it every day as a reminder.

Getting to Know You

Next we started building relationships. One of the most common situations in a larger company is that there are areas where teams feel they get stuck working at the behest of others; they feel sidelined, ignored, and looked down upon. Getting close to the legal team, the technology team, the pricing actuaries, and the operational processing folks was a big investment of time, and it required listening to debates over some pretty dry topics. But by being genuinely interested in understanding their respective predicaments, we developed positive responses.

It's also beneficial to get these folks involved in crafting the solution. One of my favorite lawyers once advised me, "Don't ask a lawyer *if* you can do something. Ask them *how* you can do something." Essentially, it boils down to respecting the other person and what they bring to the table.

With our small team's presence at meetings with these critical support teams, and by doing things as simple as summarizing outcomes, we physically demonstrated commitment. In return, they worked, and we were able to get a contract completed, build the fundamental systems infrastructure to deploy a product, complete pricing, and figure out how to administer the product if sold.

Managing Carbon Dioxide Levels

The next step was to sell. Looking at our strengths, we didn't have an established presence in the space, nor any name recognition as a stable value company.

I love the scene in the movie *Apollo 13* when one of the engineers dumps a bunch of miscellany onto the table, and says, "We gotta find a way to make this"—holds up a square-ended component—"fit into the hole for this"—holds up a smaller round-ended component—"using nothing but that"—points to materials on the table.[2] You use what you've got.

Similarly, we assessed our situation and used what we had. Though not an established player, we did have one huge advantage, one of the highest credit ratings of any company, as well as a reputation for conservatism. On top of that, being a new entrant with little experience was a compensating advantage. In this institutional space, there was a limited number of competitors, and most purchasing companies (i.e., potential customers) were near their exposure limits to the companies that had been selling to them for years. We were new, and it would be a nice addition to a buyer's balance sheet with our top quality.

But we had to get the word out.

---

2. "From Problem to Solution," *Apollo 13*, directed by Ron Howard (1995; Universal Pictures and Imagine Entertainment, 2006), DVD and Blu-ray.

I Could Tell You, But . . .

The first sale was off an old prior relationship. At a former employer, for seventeen years we had managed assets for the retirement plan of one of the US government's "alphabet soup" agencies that was on the books under a generic unidentifiable name. When one of our salespeople stumbled across their advisor and found out they were worried about the credit quality of my old employer, we proposed our higher-quality solution. After some strange tests of our resolve, including making due diligence calls over the Christmas holiday break and on the Fourth of July, we faced a final hurdle when they asked what I thought of my former employer. It was a tough line to walk. If I dissed them, I'd essentially be saying that I had put this customer in the wrong product for the last seventeen years.

I landed on saying that they'd been well-served for a number of years by a good company, but they could essentially upgrade if they moved. That honesty, representative of the prior relationship, closed the deal and gave us our first new customer.

Ramping Up

Our next challenge was growth.

Not wanting to get the head of sales upset before a sale came through, we did our second deal working on the Q.T. with one or two salespeople who were interested in the new product. Then a few more drifted in, and it came time to get his support. He had built up and sold his own companies three times and is currently working on a fourth. To do that he's had to have strong opinions, so turning him was going to be a challenge.

I first sought credibility by walking through the demand for the new product, the competitors (including those he went up against every day who didn't have it), and the facts that the new product didn't compete with existing efforts and improved profitability, all of which could make a sales team look good. I showed him one of our marketing pieces for comment, not because I needed comment but because it had my bio embedded in it, including my writing a chapter on stable value in the *Handbook of Fixed Income Investing*, a tome that many fixed income investment managers keep at their desks.

The bigger breakthrough came when I directed my now growing team to give special attention to any deals coming through from his area, even if they were small. One of them complained, "Why am I wasting my time on five and ten million-dollar deals when we have much larger prospects?"

"Because," I answered, "if we get the head of sales on our side, we open up the floodgates and have a voice supporting everything we want to do. We get resources to grow, and we get a spokesperson."

The sales head finally relented, but only if we agreed to work with a handful of salespeople who were going to hit their targets anyway and not provide the excuse of distraction to those who weren't selling much.

As we grew through several small and medium sales, our reputation did as well, and we were able to start going after bigger targets. One of the largest was a mid-Atlantic chemical company Paul had contacted on a cold call leveraging one of my old relationships. He turned it into a single jumbo sale that met our sales target all by itself. Even though I'd been working with these products for decades, when we visited the company to finalize the arrangement, they didn't look at me for assurance on open questions. Instead they turned to Paul, who'd been at it for two years. He had grown.

Growing Pains

One of the funnier issues we ran into forced me to call up some of that prior relationship-building with IT.

Our main IT contact came into my cube one day, mopping his brow and saying we had an implementation problem on the large deal Paul had just brought in.

"Really?" I asked.

"Yes. The deal's for $1.2 billion. Our systems have only enough digits to go up to $999 million."

After I stared at him for a while and finally asked, "Are you sure that's the approach you want to take on our largest sale?" he turned red and let me know that he'd go off and work on some kind of a solution. He came back with one the following week: He set up two accounts.

At $1.4 billion, the State of New York's retirement plan presented a new challenge. It's probably the most difficult contract negotiation I've been part of. They had multiple contacts at the state but had also hired a consultant (who had their own attorney) as well as an in-house state attorney and outside counsel. It took over a year to get all of them to agree with each other.

One technique that helped was that I told them upfront about Grandma's Rule (vegetables before dessert). Every time we sat down to negotiate, we went to the most difficult issues first. By the time we were in the thick of negotiations, they had adopted the expression and were starting to use it unprompted.

Because of all the volume, many with complex negotiations, we also developed a system to prioritize and manage the work, starting with a simple whiteboard listing all prospective deals, their probabilities, and next steps. There were multiple people involved, and one of the struggles was the complicated tennis match of batting documents and decisions back and forth through the organization. I tried everything I could to accelerate the process, including some of the techniques I learned in Florida such as sitting with people one-on-one and being there after hours if they were working on something, but it was still too slow given the volume.

I had modest but insufficient success redrafting a contract and sending it to one of the lawyers with my suggested wording along with, "I know I'm not a lawyer, but I've made some suggested changes. Could you comment?" While it sped the process, it was inherently disrespectful, so I finally found a solution that fit better with the relationships I wanted for myself and my team. In a precursor to what would today be called "Agile" project management, we simply got the entire team together three times a week and walked through the whiteboard, determining which deals were most important, who was doing what, and what progress we'd make by the next meeting. It's still the ideal approach.

Results

I started that stable value business in June of 2010. We wrote the first deal in December of that year, accepted a deposit in 2011, and by 2012 we had enough success that our sales target was $1.2 billion.

Big. Very big.

But that year, we did $6 billion in sales. At a prior company, it had taken me a dozen years to reach a threshold of $15 billion in assets, yet at this one we did it in three and a half.

The clincher was at the company award event celebrating the sales team's success in 2012, when the head of sales thanked us profusely from the stage and said he wouldn't have hit targets that year without us. The many proud smiles I saw while distributing Lucite mementos of a record year might have matched or exceeded the grins people had when they collected their paychecks. Setting objectives gave them something to shoot for, involving them in solving the problem conveyed ownership in the solution, demonstrating respect solidified relationships and a sense of common purpose, and ongoing prioritization got things done. Simply put, these techniques work well together.

Back in the Soup

One more example that illustrates how well these tools work comes from an operational challenge when running the investment and mutual funds area.

The job of the investment operations team was to deliver and help the company apply prices for a group of mutual funds. I took over the group at the end of May, and at the end of June we completed a planned acquisition of another company, taking the workload from 10,000 transactions a night to 120,000. As an example of the strain, we had five people in one area who were scheduled to do the work of twenty-two people at the prior company, and nobody had planned for that. In addition, we were supposed to process prices by 5 a.m. or risk having to reimburse partner companies for losses and create a ton of rework. We had routinely been processing by 1 a.m., but after the acquisition we often missed the 5 a.m. deadline. To top it off, we were putting in a brand-new set of systems changes at the same time.

The resulting initial environment was a disaster, with people sleeping or crying at their desks at four in the morning, everyone calling in favors with the mutual fund providers so we wouldn't incur losses, and the systems work being behind schedule. The head of my operations team once literally had five scheduled meetings on her calendar during the same one-hour block.

If I hadn't faced something similar to this problem before, I would've been horrified. Having been through the Florida turnaround didn't make this turnaround easy, but it gave us a path.

Many Small Steps Again

I repeated some of the same things we'd done in Florida, starting as described by arriving with goodies from the local wholesale club during the evening and sitting with the team as they worked through issues. I then divided the workload between routine processing and systems development. My operations leader, for example, had been responsible for (and capable of) both but didn't have the bandwidth, so I gave the systems work to someone else. She initially complained about the change, saying I was taking something away from her, but I asked for her faith and let her know this would let her do one thing really well. After that, we got all the affected areas together at once to walk through the process so that they'd all understand each other's roles and dependencies, and we shortened the number of steps required. Key leaders used "office hours" and "do not disturb" times to limit interruption and to focus, and for monitoring we started by tracking the basics. For instance, when we had some summer staff come in to help clean up a backlog and they didn't have a tracking system for their work, we put up a paper flip chart with their names on it and gave them each a different colored marker, and that's what we used.

I found our operations lead in tears one day and asked what was wrong. She said her daughter was graduating from college on

Long Island, but she couldn't go because she wouldn't leave her team in the lurch. Even after urging her that the team could cover for her, she wouldn't give up on the need to be accessible (don't ask your team to do anything you wouldn't do). So, we paid for a car service for her and her daughter. That let her be accessible while with her daughter for an important event, and she found she didn't have to be available every second.

We also gave autonomy to the teams doing the work. For example, we had a night team composed of entry-level processors ranging from ages eighteen to twenty-seven, and one more experienced woman in her mid- to late-sixties. Most people would consider the team's work pretty mundane and boring; they got faxes or emails every night, at different times and in different formats, from all our mutual funds. One young lady went through a pink highlighter (her favorite color) every few nights, underlining the relevant section before handing it to someone else for input into the computer.

When we talked with the night team about process improvement, the first few things they did were small. The first was to move a wastebasket closer. Another was to start posting their release times on a whiteboard every night. A few days after these modest improvements, I got an email requesting approval for a "grabber" to use when the photocopier jammed. It was $15.99 on Amazon. I approved it with a (mostly tongue-in-cheek) message that if they ever asked me for approval on something like that again instead of just ordering it, I'd fire somebody. They bought it.

Turns out the copier was going down multiple times a night, taking staff thirty to forty-five minutes to unjam it every time it did. With the grabber, they could remove the jam in a matter of seconds. It's not as good as fixing the copier (we did) or making the transaction electronic so it wouldn't need copies (they eventually did), but it was what we needed at the time. After the grabber came in, I got an email with a short video of it being used, along with the caption "Worth its weight in gold!"

Turning Over a New Leaf

I was hit with a gut punch one day when a survey asking whether the investment team understood strategy came back with dismal results, even after I'd spent many hours walking the floor and explaining it. Then I remembered a lesson from Florida: Involve the team.

I picked four members from a group of volunteers and charged them with finding a way to get across our strategic imperatives. They came up with the creative approach of putting up a poster of a tree with the roots representing our values and the trunk being our strategic initiatives. There was also an individual leaf for each person with their picture on it (mandatory), a description of what they did, and something important to them.

When they showed it to me, my reaction was similar to the one I'd had to the AAA mnemonic. Although it looked hokey, if it was what they wanted to do, they should push ahead with it. Only they weren't thinking big enough. I agreed to pay to have it reprinted at four times the size, and we unveiled it with a ceremony where we planted a real tree outside the window where the team worked. That effort not only clarified the importance of strategy with the team but brought them together. The four even ran a contest to see who best described on their leaves what they did for the company. The prizes were based on the things they'd identified as important, so we gave away a donation to an animal shelter, a pirate cruise for somebody and their kids, and a new iPad to someone whose motto was "Automate everything."

Results

This combination of steps, in total, was a huge success.

Processing came back not just from post-5 a.m. to pre-5 a.m., nor even to pre-acquisition 1 a.m., but to before midnight. The record time on the night team's whiteboard was 10:20 p.m.

My operations lead stopped by one morning to tell me she was glad we split the two jobs apart: "I realized I'm really good at operations, and I like fixing things." She then ran downstairs, excited to deal with an issue.

The night team automated their process, and most of them went on to bigger jobs, one running a reconciliation team, one leading multimillion-dollar systems projects, and one becoming treasurer of our mutual funds.

When the CEO surprised us early one morning with a "walk-around" visit, the only person there was Sue, the lead of the council of four who had figured out how to convey our strategy, and she sat right by the 8' x 8' tree the team had developed. After she not only provided a clear explanation of strategy but shared the motivation it had generated for the team, the CEO was heard on multiple future surprise visits to all corners of the company closing with, "Where's your tree?"

> ***Tools for solving business problems, motivating people, and improving processes work effectively in multiple real-world situations.***

Summary

Larger challenges can be approached the same way as smaller ones. Keep these additional tools in mind, whether fixing an existing problem or growing a new business:

- *Break problems into chunks.*
- *Immerse yourself in the business and issue, end to end.*
- *Be visible. Engage employees at all levels.*
- *Find and remove bottlenecks.*
- *Look first for simple fixes that address the biggest issues.*
- *Set an objective.*
- *Beg, borrow, and steal resources.*
- *Build a network of relationships, including helping others with what they care about.*
- *Find a shared approach to track and reprioritize everything.*
- *Motivate the team.*

Wing to Wing

Although the topics and skills we've considered so far are meaningful throughout a career, three specialty areas take on particular prominence as we rise in an organization. They often involve higher stakes, sometimes the future of an entire organization, and may require a senior leader to take a view and drive to a decision. Interestingly, they fall into three buckets: one around ensuring consistent positive growth, one that protects against disaster, and one that balances pluses and minuses to evolve a company.

- Chapter 12 defines innovation and what it takes to succeed at it and offers some techniques to apply it.
- Chapter 13 examines risk management.
- Chapter 14 walks through negotiation tactics and strategies.

Chapter 12

What's New? (Innovation)

One of the biggest work challenges I've run into started with a positive, the best job offer I've ever gotten.

Out for pizza together, one of my favorite bosses, also named Brian, asked how things were going. "Good," I told him, "but I'm getting bored doing the same thing over and over for fourteen years. I'd like to do something different, more cutting edge."

"Okay," he said. "Good performance review."

If you didn't know Brian well, you might have thought he was brushing me off. He wasn't. We didn't need much more conversation because we talked frequently. It wasn't a complete surprise, then, when two weeks later the head of our retirement business, who later went on to head personal lines at the nation's largest mutual fund, offered me a new job.

"Brian," she said (speaking to me rather than to him), "our competitors are out there doing a bunch of different things. I'm not really sure what's going on. You're my new head of innovation. Take a couple of people, go off in a corner, and come back in a year and tell me what we should do."

What made the offer so good was that it was so open-ended. It was also daunting to move from something I knew really well and had a good track record for to something new and undefined.

In this chapter, we'll cover the following questions:

- *What is innovation and why do we need it?*
- *How is disruptive innovation different?*
- *How do I gather information about what customers need in order to guide innovation efforts?*
- *How do I gather support for innovation and overcome organizational biases against it?*
- *How do I structure and interact with teams to encourage innovation?*
- *What techniques promote innovative thinking?*
- *Once I have a lot of ideas, how do I narrow them down and ensure execution?*

What Is Innovation, and Why Should a Senior Leader Care?

Fittingly, my team of three and I were the first four people in a new building and started, as with any new responsibility, with immersion. We quickly absorbed as much as we could about the many types of innovation, small and large. Every time somebody makes a process improvement, even the night team moving a wastebasket closer, that's a small innovation.

We hadn't been broken out as a separate area to do small things, so we focused on one end of the spectrum called "disruptive (or breakthrough) innovation," something that fundamentally changes the rules and status quo whether in technology, service, or customer experience and relationships. An early surprise about this type of innovation completely flipped my prior notion that innovation is top-down. I'd always thought that you see what your biggest customers are looking for, develop that to keep them happy, then take a streamlined version of it down market at scale.

That view is flawed at its core and is the exact opposite of what you want to do.

For one thing, your largest customers are not representative of other buyers. They have resources that smaller buyers don't have, they can pay for bells and whistles, and very often they not only want but demand customization that smaller buyers can't use or don't care about. Their evaluation capabilities are different, their budgets are larger, and they're generally less nimble and have trouble changing. In short, your largest customers are different from your small buyers.

In retrospect, I should've seen the distinction from my own experience. In retirement and financial services, for instance, we customized big and small items for our largest customers, such as specialized communication brochures and separate dedicated phone lines. For relationship management, we worked with their separate benefits department rather than with someone who meets with you for half an hour in between resolving some manufacturing issue and finding coverage for an employee who didn't show up that morning. The specialization and handholding you provide to big customers is not easily replicable.

I confirmed that big customers can also be a pain in the neck when I attended a conference with fifty or so of our top third-party administrators, firms who keep track of retirement records on behalf of companies. They demonstrated a striking pattern when I asked them about their business. Most of the group described having several smaller customers but one really big one who was a pain to deal with, requiring constant support and costing them money. A few who didn't complain described having been in the same situation but firing the big customer and improving profits, personal health, and vacation time.

Sure, big customers can cover a lot of fixed costs and support an R&D budget, but they're not a source of new ideas that will translate to a mass audience. That's why innovation expert Clayton Christensen is able to provide multiple reinforcing examples that innovation isn't top-down but bottom-up. One in the steel industry stands out. Smaller companies entered the market with low-end, less profitable, lower-quality product, only to be ignored by large, established competitors who said things like, "That's not a part of the market we want anyway. It's all low-quality stuff. We're losing money on it. Let them have it." The smaller competitors, still ignored, gradually improved quality, and by the time they'd taken over a big chunk of the market were too successful for the larger companies to defend themselves against, in a space they used to dominate.

Big steel producers are just one example. There's a litany of well-known companies that went under because of a failure to innovate, including Buggy Whip manufacturers, Kodak's and Polaroid's film businesses, Blockbuster, Blackberry, and Borders. The common factor is failing to keep up as the game elementally changes.

Many years ago, I came across one analogous explanation in a science magazine article about extinction, particularly regarding why smaller animals outlived many larger species. Suppose animals are competing for food. They grow larger and larger to crowd out the other animals or get better and better at predation. Through generations, they enhance their strength, getting bigger or faster and developing a competitive advantage. Then something changes, like say, a drought or famine. Each individual large animal now needs much more to survive. An organism that has been adapted to compete based on size now has size as a disadvantage. It needs to eat, and eat a lot. Smaller organisms may die individually, but there are lots of them, and each can survive on small amounts. Bye-bye dinosaurs, hello cockroaches.

Large corporations are similar. They have a hard time adapting to change. A market downturn in financial services is an example of one such change. Financial services firms take a big hit to profits as their revenues go down but their expenses stay up due to their size and fixed nature. They try to manage through it with painful layoffs but are limited because you can't lay off a building or downsize an existing technology stack. In that environment, you also become more dependent on those large customers, even lousy ones, because their revenues cover a lot of your expenses. Maintaining innovation then becomes existential.

There's one advantage that a corporation has over an animal though. It's made of component parts. A brontosaurus can't say to its left foreleg, "Go off and innovate for a year," but a large company can, if it has the foresight and courage to do it.

 *Large established companies need to innovate to protect themselves and to do so by learning what their smaller customers collectively need.* 

Not Sure What I'm Having Yet

"Great! So, how do I learn what those customers need?"

Asking that question led to a second surprise: You can ask them, and they'll have an opinion, but *they don't know.*

If you want to discover what a customer needs, don't ask them. Just like process improvement and motivating people, watch them in real time or get as close to that as possible.

I had a friend and colleague who'd done work for a large manufacturer of accounting software for small businesses, one that ultimately had about 90 percent market share and recently advertised for the finals of the NBA and both the European and Copa America soccer championships. He said he spent the first year of development looking over the shoulders of small business owners and observing how they used their existing software. He asked himself questions like, "When do they get frustrated and yell and scream at the screen? When do they create a workaround because the way the system does it isn't effective? When do they get excited, stand up, and yell 'Yes!' at the top of their lungs?" That's how you tell what your customer cares about and what needs to change.

I had the luxury of presenting to Google and asking for critique during our time innovating. The one thing I remember most clearly is a comment after the presentation: "I don't claim to know the financial services industry, but you're on the right track as long as you keep trying to understand the customer."

 **To learn about your customers, watch them.** 

I'm Not Comfortable with That

Even when you realize where to focus your innovation efforts, you can't make progress until you find a way as a leader to overcome an organization's complacency bias, the idea that "We've been doing it this way for years. We do it right. We have top market share. Let's not put that all at risk by changing everything that's worked." It's generals trying to fight the last war.

After I spoke with him about such bias, the head of innovation for one of the country's largest and most successful consulting firms prefaced his advice to me with this: "That bias will always be there. You have reams of data on your existing business, and that data gives confidence that even a small change with your existing book is predictable and manageable. It may not be true, but you have to deal with it. New is scary." His advice was threefold:

1. You need top-level support, meaning the CEO. We had close to that from the US head of our business; it wasn't complete, but it was strong. We saw just how strong when she left and her successor disbanded the unit after it had been running for only eighteen months.

2. Find supporters in unlikely places. The head of finance usually doesn't get to dream up new ideas, they just report things quarterly. Heads of IT and operations usually just execute what somebody else came up with, so they feel second class. When I pulled our CFO in upfront and asked for her opinions, I got an incredible level of support, and a budget.

3. As much as you can, separate innovation efforts from the rest of your business. You need a dedicated team of resources, not people working off the sides of their desks. You also need a separate and meaningful budget. Ideally, you want a separate location and even culture.

I'll add one warning on the third point, based on a mistake I made. I was so enamored of the separateness that I didn't pull in the business heads of the existing lines early and often enough for updates and support. I got it from their teams, which was awesome, but I needed it from the heads of those areas. If I did it over again, I'd spend more time selling internally.

There's a useful technique for any time you're trying to convince someone of something in an organization, especially for things like innovation that are new and different. Remember that you have more tools than just logic to convince someone. We probably spend 90–95 percent of our time arguing with or trying to convince someone of a course of action based on what approach is most rational, such as developing projected earnings spreadsheets. That just tends to get the person you're arguing with to dig in their heels more deeply. In the world of innovation, tap into your additional sources of obtaining buy-in, namely emotion and audience connection.

If you've appropriately focused on the customer, letting them demonstrate their emotion around a topic is usually more impactful than being passionate about it yourself, though both can work. A video of a focus group participant yelling, "I just don't understand what I'm supposed to do here!" or "All these companies want to do is make a buck off of you, and this proves it!" is powerful.

In chapter 4, I mentioned how a locally produced low-cost video generated a better response from our audience than a professionally produced one, because it connected. You can do the same thing with an internal audience. Find out what they care about, and shop your idea around first to get buy-in from key decision-makers before a big meeting.

 ***Align your organization for innovative success.*** 

Where Am I?

Once you've got your infrastructure for innovation established, it's important for anyone participating in new efforts to understand what phase you're in.

Early in Gerard Puccio's *The Creative Thinker's Toolkit*, he makes a distinction between divergent and convergent thinking. Divergent thinking is like brainstorming, when you come up with a lot of different ideas. That's the area where you might get people together from different backgrounds, throw out a ton of different possibilities, and take the approach of "There's no bad idea." In other words, you build on each other. Convergent thinking, by comparison, is narrowing your list down to a handful of items so that you can do something about them. It's tough and hard-nosed, but that's so you can direct limited available resources to those prospects with the highest likelihood of success.

It's important to explicitly recognize which of these stages you're in. Are you brainstorming, the phase in which there's no bad idea, or are you in the narrowing phase, when you need to be strict and make hard decisions?

> **Being explicit and upfront about the objectives of the stage you're in helps frame conversations.**

To Infinity, or at Least in That Direction

In 1968, the *Apollo 8* spacecraft carried the first crew with a mission to orbit the moon. NASA was in its heyday, and a long line of smart people wanted to work there. The application process was tough, testing multiple measures. One such test was in the area of creativity.

That same year, researcher George Land initiated a study on creativity. Because of its rigor, he chose the same creativity test NASA used in its vetting process, and when he applied it to four different groups he got a shockingly wide disparity of results:

When you do, it's important to foster a safe, open space where the goal is to generate ideas, not judge them. Let the team know you're in the brainstorming phase, and encourage everyone to share their ideas aloud while ensuring quieter voices are heard. Respect the flow of conversation, allowing one speaker at a time and ensuring everyone has a chance to contribute.

You want to create an environment for collaboration by building on the ideas of others, so encourage the team to embrace all ideas, even those that seem unconventional or incomplete, and praise the creative thinking behind them. Because you have diverse personalities in the room, some will want to immediately jump to saying things like, "That will never work" or "We've tried that before." Ask them to set aside their disbelief, and assure them you will come back to their concerns once you've generated a long list of ideas.

Before you jump into brainstorming itself, I've found one other exercise extremely useful, and it takes patience. List the problems your customer has, identifying them from direct observation rather than guessing or even asking. As noted earlier, customers don't always know what they want, but they do know what bothers them. Once you have your list of customer problems, prioritize it. Without thinking through solutions yet, and especially not thinking through viability yet, determine what things are bothering your customers the most. Then you can start brainstorming solutions knowing what you're solving for.

 *Assemble a diverse team for brainstorming, and set it up for success.* 

Wall? What Wall?

With the group united, briefed, aware of the ground rules and expectations, and focused on the highest priority customer problems, here are some approaches that have worked to enhance innovation:

1. Restate

The restate approach can be as simple as going around the room and having everyone restate the problem in their own words.

I saw the following scene play out once when we used this approach: One person was looking for the most accurate answer for the customer. Another wanted the most trustworthy and reliable answer, even if not accurate. Yet a third thought the customer wanted a quick and easy answer. Depending on which of those three paths you take, you generate wildly different solutions.

A variation of this is to restate the objective, usually in more specific terms. For example, instead of asking "How do we reduce errors?" describe the objective as "How do we reduce deposit errors from six percent to two percent by June 30?" Strangely, more specific constraints generate greater creativity than a broad description.

2. Go to Extremes

There was an unsourced story making the rounds of the innovation circuit a few decades ago. Despite its dated subject matter, it's still relevant for breakthrough thinking.

Back in the days when Blockbuster was emerging as the king of video rentals, two business owners of a local rental shop were contemplating going under. As a last-ditch effort, they asked themselves an extreme question: "What if we were to charge zero dollars for rentals?"

On the surface, this seems a ludicrous question, but it led to a creative response. They needed an alternative source of revenue, so they did make a limited supply of a handful of videos free of charge, but they placed them at the back of the store. Customers would walk through the store and see other videos they liked, and those who arrived early enough to get the free rentals paid to rent a second or third one, while those who didn't shrugged their shoulders and rented a paid one instead. The owners also placed by the register some pricier goods with higher margins, such as gourmet popcorn, chocolate, and wine. They survived. At least for a while.

Another approach is to imagine that a new competitor comes into your market and has unlimited resources. I've often encouraged MBA classes to think through how they would improve the check-in process at a hotel if they didn't have limits on their expenses. The first few responses are usually tepid: "Add more people at the front desk" or "Bring a customer's luggage upstairs for free." After I get them to open up, we often land at something like this: "We meet you at the airport with our limo. There's no luggage to collect because we've bought you all new outfits, in your sizes and styles, and they're pressed and waiting for you in your room. You've already been checked in, and we'll escort you to your room. Your favorite snacks are waiting for you, and your massage is scheduled for tomorrow at 5 p.m., before dinner."

We don't have unlimited resources, but this exercise gets us thinking in extremes. The next step is to ask which of these efforts most delight the customer and why. Then you can get your hands on some ideas that are attainable.

3. Reverse Psychometry

On a trip to Chile, my colleagues in Santiago were looking for a way to reduce the enrollment time for a new product. They used the worst-answer approach, which works like this: How could we make it harder for a customer to sign up with us?

This was a very customer-focused group, and at the outset they struggled with the idea of making a problem worse. But at the end of the session, they were describing all kinds of creative hurdles given free rein, including "You have to get sign-off from your childhood priest, and the forms are all in ancient Greek" and "You have to stand on a chair and sing your answers," the latter of which one of them proceeded to do.

The next step was to assess what it was about that description that was most annoying to a customer and why and then reverse the process. This group came up with an approach where they developed five personas, each looking to buy the product, and each coming with a backstory including age, job, family life, and hobbies. In their materials, they then showed which option that imaginary customer elected and why. Over 85 percent of buyers chose a premixed package identical to one chosen by a persona. By making signing up simpler and with fewer steps, they got the enrollment time down to a matter of hours.

4. Now We're Cookin'

The professor for one innovation class in which I guest-lectured gave an assignment of designing a new backyard grill within a stated budget. The students had pushed traditional innovation techniques about as far as they could. One, for example, was a morphological approach, a fancy way of saying changing the size, shape, color, or other characteristic of the thing you're designing.

Instead, I asked them to think through the primary purpose of the shopper in buying the grill. What was the job of the grill, and what résumé did it need? This brought them a much broader set of answers. If the buyer's objective is to show off their artistry, maybe include a variety of color-coded spatulas with the grill, each with the griller's name on it, along with matching hooks for them to hang from. If the deck where the grill is located is a gathering spot, maybe mark the grill with a small magnet for each person there. If grilling is instead an oasis of seclusion, maybe find just one spot for the cook's beer. And if the grill is a fancy decoration for the deck, maybe make it look like a classic automobile.

> **_Try a variety of specific and tested techniques_**
> **_to increase idea generation._**

Get the Red Out

One framework for thinking through disruptive innovation opportunities integrates well with those step-by-step techniques. In their book *Blue Ocean Strategy*, W. Chan Kim and Renée Mauborgne champion the innovative ideas found in the open space of the blue ocean, as distinct from the red ocean left figuratively bloodied as competitors prey on each other with wars based on price, commission, or product features. They provide the examples of a wine company that priced themselves between a fiercely competitive beer market and high-end wines based on snob appeal and tasting scores, and a renowned traveling aerial troupe priced between in-person movies and a professional theater show.

Similarly, Amazon developed a laser focus on choice and convenience versus the traditional focus on personal local service. And ING Direct, one of the first successful online banks, decided to forgo competing on traditional elements such as banking hours, ATMs, and cross-selling insurance or retirement advice and invested the savings from those large expenses in crediting a high interest rate on savings accounts. They offered a rate ten times the national average and broke even in about four years instead of the seven built into their plan.

> *Reduce the focus of your offerings from those areas in which competition is most intense, and redeploy the expense savings to features customers care about.*

Less Is Also More

Once you've generated a presumably long list of ideas, your work is not complete. You're now ready for the hard part, narrowing things down.

Nobody likes to narrow because, once again, it involves giving something up, and we're terminally loss-averse. Yet this is the most critical part of the process, so I'll ask you to keep a few things in mind. Just as in the brainstorming phase, you're likely to run into resistance, this time in the opposite direction with comments like, "It's such a good idea. I don't want to give up on it. It'll work." Similar to naysayers during brainstorming, you can usually get this group to continue by letting them know they'll have another shot at making a case later. Here's how:

- Use data whenever it's available.
- Recognize that for new initiatives, detailed information such as profit margins or sales projections may be limited or nonexistent.

- Base your insights on customer frustrations and pain points, using their own words whenever possible.
- Avoid substituting your opinion for the customer's. Their perspective is what truly counts.
- Apply prioritization and decision-making techniques to identify where to concentrate your efforts.
- Let the most critical customer problems guide your focus.

> ***Narrow your list so you can execute a few ideas well.***

Still Not Done Yet

The last step in the innovation process is trying things out and seeing whether they work. Your prioritized ideas won't be perfect, but get them out into the market, usually on a small scale so that you can test first and then adjust. To do that, you'll need to measure results, and it's good to establish success measures and objectives before you start.

When we were developing alliances at one firm to help customers better manage their debt, we looked at both student loan refinance and home mortgage refinance. Carefully vetting partners for both, we selected a heavily advertised household name for mortgage refinance and a smaller, lesser known but nimbler partner for student loans. Then we piloted both.

Our initial metric, volume of business written, didn't reveal much. However, through conversations with insurance agents who spoke directly with customers, we found a better indicator. Customers showed little interest in mortgage refinancing but were quickly engaged by the potential savings from reducing student loan debt. One agent recalled a conversation with a prospective client, a new doctor fresh out of residency. She was literally staring at her hands, worried about what would happen to her income if she lost their use: "I really want to buy this policy, but I can't afford it. I have too much student loan debt."

Doctors and dentists tend to carry the highest student loan debt, with dentists especially facing costs close to half a million dollars to set up their practices, and both professions often focus so heavily on work that they don't even know their loan interest rates. In this doctor's case, refinancing her student loans lowered her rate by more than 5 percent, freeing enough cash to purchase the disability policy. The agent was ecstatic.

Armed with this insight, we pivoted our efforts to focus on student loans.

 ***Test your new products to see what works, and adjust as necessary.*** 

A Quick Case Study

Financial providers have long struggled to encourage people to invest more for their retirement, mostly because it requires a behavior change to give up something today in order to have more on hand far down the road. There are also issues of trust with large organizations, and significant operational hurdles. Companies have experimented with a variety of approaches over decades, from increasingly sophisticated projection tools, to simplified messaging, to automatic investment features.

To address the issue, our innovation team pulled together a cross-organizational group, enumerated and prioritized customer problems, brainstormed 140 different potential solutions, and prioritized the list down to a top three, which we tested in the market. The one that worked best allowed people to compare how much they saved, as well as other financial metrics, to other people like them. Not only did it show a propensity to increase savings, but it provided new insights into customer preferences and thought processes. The company still maintains a modified version of the new tool today.

Summary

Innovation requires its own mindset and approaches:

- *Disruptive or breakthrough innovation is bottom-up, not top-down.*
- *Customers don't know what they need. To find out, watch them instead of asking them.*
- *Separate your innovation efforts with a high level of sponsorship and support to align your organization around innovation.*
- *Sell ideas both internally and externally, and use emotion and connection in addition to logic.*
- *During innovation, be aware of self-limitations and whether you're in the divergent (open-ended) or convergent (narrowing down) phase.*

- *Use intentional techniques to break through natural barriers to creativity and new ideas.*
- *Before starting, prepare for brainstorming, placing a high focus on the customer and assembling a diverse team.*
- *To generate new ideas, consider restating, going to extremes, reversing the problem, or determining jobs to be done.*
- *Zig where others zag, meaning reduce your focus on areas where the competition is most intense and use the savings to differentiate.*
- *Be both process- and customer-driven as you narrow your priorities.*
- *Pilot, measure, monitor, and pivot your innovation efforts.*

Chapter 13

Watch Out! (Managing Risk)

Risk is another specialized area with its own lexicon and mindset. It's critical in finance, insurance, and investments, which are my backgrounds, but with today's integration of virtually all businesses with the financial markets, it's important to manufacturers and service companies as well. Risk touches everything in an organization. It's half of every decision. We compare the risk and the reward and see whether one is worth the other. Risk is integrated with all other aspects of running a company, and a single misfire on risk can take a company under.

In this chapter, we'll cover the following questions:

- *How do I handle organizational reluctance to engage in risk discussions?*
- *Which risks should I avoid, and which should I take?*
- *What are some common ways risks manifest, and how can I protect against them?*
- *What red flags alert me to potential unseen risks?*
- *How can I make those in the organization who focus on risk the most effective?*

Half the Equation

There's a danger (should I say a risk?) in focusing on risk as its own discipline because it represents only one side of the equation, the negative. Since most companies are focused on the positive side of the equation, such as increasing market share and earnings, talking about risk can make an organization uncomfortable.

Over forty years ago, psychologists Daniel Kahneman and Amos Tversky described the effect of framing on how people make decisions. A simple example is this:

A. 95 percent of patients who have this operation survive.

B. 5 percent of the patients who have this operation die.

Many more study participants chose option A, framed in the positive, than B, framed negatively.

Risk tends to frame problems in the negative: "Which of these would you most like to avoid?" This is largely the same challenge we discussed in chapter 7. We're naturally inclined to look at the negative and imagine all the bad things that might happen. If instead you use the "As if" method, treating your decision as if it's already been made or an event as if it's already happened, things become more balanced. Objects appear smaller in the rear-view mirror than they did at the time.

Because we're naturally loss-averse, we have a much deeper emotional response to a negative outcome than we do to a positive outcome of the same magnitude. Not all risks are the same. I often reminded my risk team that as Chief Risk Officer, I had, and therefore they had, two jobs:

1. Avoid disaster. Don't take the company under or injure it to such a state of disrepair that it's limping along. Do that by considering unrecoverable risks.
2. For smaller risks, provide information that helps people make better decisions. Not perfect decisions, but better decisions.

One tool to skirt the negative-only view is to keep these two categories in mind and think about which bucket you're in at the moment. That way, you're less likely to treat a molehill like a mountain.

In either case, it's valuable to engage multiple perspectives, which results in multiple framing. The operations team will consider different aspects of a decision than will sales, and the finance area will have a different view than law, the CEO, or marketing. A full view of risk requires diversity.

> ***Differentiate risk decisions, consider different ways to frame risk, and gather diverse input.***

Baking Cookies

Let's look at an example of what I mean by an unrecoverable risk.

My wife and I awoke one morning to the sound of clanging metal in the kitchen and the smell of smoke. I rushed downstairs and found our daughter, then about eight years old, standing in front of the oven door. She had seen her mother bake some delicious chocolate chip cookies the day before and, in an attempt to emulate her, had mixed up a batch of batter, including the key ingredients of butter, sugar, and chocolate chips but leaving out others, such as flour. She'd then cranked up the oven dial to the max.

After we got the fire alarm off, we had a discussion: "Honey, I really want you to be able to experiment with different recipes and try things out,"—she looked at me eagerly—"but don't burn the house down."

She never repeated the dangerous approach of that day, has experimented with cooking all her life, and has developed several new and delicious recipes.

> ***Simply put, don't put at risk something that you can't afford to lose.***

Better Smart than Lucky

A familiar example of a bridge too far from business is Lehman Brothers, a formerly high-rated Wall Street firm that went belly up during the 2008 global financial crisis. They never recovered from investing too much in and betting on bad residential mortgages.

Even when a company survives such large risks, they should've avoided them in the first place. Just because they didn't go under doesn't mean they couldn't have. The London Whale, a single trader for JP Morgan, cost the firm $6 billion in trading losses and another $1 billion in penalties in 2012. It didn't swamp the company, but that's a crazy big number.

During the 1987 crash, the company I worked for had $19 billion in an investment product called "portfolio insurance," which was intended to give investors part of the upside if stocks went up but limit the downside. During the height of the trading day on October 19, deemed "Black Monday," our head trader registered two massively different stock index values on his trading screen, and with the president looking over his shoulder he guessed which was correct and hit a button. He guessed right, and the company never lost a dime for themselves or their customers, but the trader could've guessed wrong.

The business examples of open-ended unrecoverable risk may seem distant unless you work or worked for one of those companies. They take on more import when you think of them at a personal level. A buddy and I, for instance, almost got hypothermia during an October hike up Mt. Adams in the White Mountains. I'd heard stories about how dangerous it can get atop the wind-blasted ridges in the Whites, even that early in the year. Still, it was sunny and warm as we left the campground at the bottom and got directly onto the trail, and we were sweating after half an hour. Fresh from reading a book about deaths in these mountains, I had at least partially prepared, with decent hiking clothes, good boots, and jackets in our packs. At the last second, I'd also thrown in two extra pairs of socks in case ours got wet. But I hadn't counted on how deceptively cold it would be on the mountain top.

When we emerged from the tree line, the point above which only low scrub grows in the rocks because of altitude and exposure, we encountered a light drizzle. Though I remembered that hypothermia sneaks up on you, we felt great and sensed no danger. Nevertheless, something must have tugged at my subconscious because I made one of the wiser decisions in my life: setting limits in advance. My friend and I agreed that we'd hike one hour up and over the ridge. If after that we hadn't reached the Madison Springs hut, a shelter with heat and likely some warm soup, we'd head back down.

When we reached the appointed limit, still feeling good but chilly, I attempted to reach into my pack to pull out the extra socks for us to use as mittens. I was surprised to find that I couldn't even bring my fingers together to grasp the zipper on the pack and had to squeeze together my palms to get inside it. We somehow got the socks onto our hands, then turned around hoping we'd make it back below the tree line.

After an interminable hour, including clapping our hands together and moving as quickly as we could without falling, we were within sight of the tree line through the fog ahead. My friend sat down, pack still on, and insisted he couldn't go any further. I unsuccessfully cajoled and yelled at him, then tried lifting him, and in desperation I extracted his pack, moved it partway down the path, and came back. With both our packs off, I was finally able to stand him up, and we stumbled forward to the shelter of the trees where we recovered some strength. After re-shouldering our packs, we picked our way down carefully, aware that we might not have our full faculties about us.

We finally reached camp and found it even warmer than when we'd left. After four hours of me apologizing for putting my friend in that position, neither of us had frostbite and both of us could snap our fingers again.

Dying from hypothermia, even in one of my favorite places, was an unrecoverable risk.

What can we do about these largest risks, the ones that can cause death or serious injury whether of an individual or of a company, without getting so focused on them that we can't think of anything else? Setting limits, like the timeframe for turning around on the top of Mt. Adams, worked, but it almost didn't. So here's a corollary when using limits to protect against existential risk: Be extremely reluctant to vary from the limit you set. To ensure compliance, make the decision to change your mind a joint one with multiple parties.

>  ***For large risks, set limits in advance and stick to them.*** 

That's Cray-Cray

A valuable approach to managing risk is to understand how one might manifest. If you can understand how it could happen, then you can both identify when you're approaching danger and protect against it.

In the early days of super-computing and before laptops became as powerful as they are today, a fixed income investment team rented out space on a Cray-2 to run and dissect ten thousand path-dependent scenarios.

"What do you do with the data when you get it back?" I asked.

"Well, we take the average and use that as our risk measure," said one portfolio manager.

One of his savvier colleagues interrupted with a more practical approach: "Out of ten thousand scenarios, you look at the ten or twenty that are the worst results. Then you pick those apart to see if they have anything in common, how they would occur."

In a similar vein, what-if exercises help define what might happen and in a much more useful way than the theory alone that I've seen in some risk plans. My risk team, two weeks prior to the COVID-19 shutdown and before I started working with them, ran a test sending people home to see whether they could work remotely in the event of a major storm or other disruption. They found and made corrections as simple as ensuring people took their computers with them when they left for the day. While you might laugh about how obvious that is, when COVID-19 hit they were up and running the next day while other companies took weeks.

Similar real-world tests around cybersecurity risks or a potential banking or commercial real estate crisis helped the company avoid what could've caused significant damage.

> ***Try to figure out how a risk will arise so that you can do something about it.***

Monsters on Tiptoe

One particularly insidious and common risk is the one that arises from gradually increased exposure.

I can't remember the first time I heard the "frog in the pot" metaphor, but I know I've run into it about a hundred times. Still, like most trite aphorisms, it has a ring of truth. The idea is that if you put a frog in a pot of boiling water it will jump out, but if you turn up the temp gradually it will die.

I don't know whether that's really what happens with frogs and if it does who was sadistic enough to conduct the experiment, but I can tell you it happens in real life. At one company, we had a huge portfolio of GICs, the CD-type institutional investments I mentioned are used by pension funds. When one day I sat with the actuary who was monitoring the portfolio's risk, he bragged about how well-diversified the investments were and about the sophisticated risk measures we had in place. His team had even modeled a scenario twice as bad as the Great Depression.

A few years later, the company took an almost $1 billion write-off on the business and had to stop selling it. The cause? First, although the portfolio was well-diversified, we owned about 50 percent more of the bad investments than the rest of the industry did. Second, the scenario that occurred was actually about *four* times as bad as the Great Depression. We'd missed the forest while looking carefully at each tree.

What happened? Successive investment committees seeking just a tad more return each time they met added risk in such small increments that any one increase seemed insignificant. Added up over the years, though, they'd taken on much more risk than they'd realized, and it cost the company a lot of money.

An amplifying effect with gradual risk is that when the inevitable crisis occurs that exposes you to substantial cumulative risk, everything goes bad at once. In this case, the risk manager's extensive diversification had provided only the illusion of protection because the risk that occurred was endemic to the entire portfolio.

What could the company have done differently in this case? Sticking to limits would've helped. Multiple perspectives or a fresh look at risk tolerance in total rather than incrementally, or at what portfolio-level risks might occur, also could've offered some protection.

> ***Watch out for risks that accumulate slowly,***
> ***and periodically incorporate fresh views***
> ***to protect against them.***

People Are Strange

Don't overlook the human side of risk.

In the governmental market, I've seen some of the best customer relationships go south when there's a change in administration or key personnel after an election. When this happens, nonfinancial risk turns into financial risk.

A solution is to maintain relationships at multiple levels within an external organization. Similarly, if you look at where in your own organization your associates tend to make exceptions or break the rules, that's a strong signal that something isn't working and a good hint of an underlying risk. As with process improvement, direct visual observation at the ground level is a much more effective way to spot a risk than a theoretical model. Look at actual deals or transactions.

Another people-related risk is hiring a bunch of staff because they think and act like you. You need diversity in your team. Critically, that's not enough. The environment needs to be one where everyone is willing to speak up and contribute their points of view.

 **Be aware of the human element of risk.** 

You're Out of Line!

Misalignment of objectives is another cause of risk.

I once sent one of my process experts to figure out why a systems project kept getting delayed. He came back after a short time and said it was because they had to run so many tests and as of yet had completed only about twenty out of eighty.

"Keep digging," I said.

He did, and a week later he came back laughing.

"What did you find out?" I asked.

"You really want to know?"

"Yes."

"They get paid based on how many tests they perform."

We changed the structure, and they implemented successfully a few months later, executing about twenty-five tests.

In another example, a technology project migrated from about $60 million of projected costs and a one-year projected timeframe to being abandoned at $400 million after seven years. Misalignment on compensation and intellectual property was again a driver, along with other causes. There were signs of misalignment if you looked for them. During a low point on the effort, a colleague helped uncover that one of the high-level IT folks had yelled at his team for inviting a project manager to a meeting: "I don't want them to know what we're doing!"

That's not alignment.

Here's an example that is. Somebody who was cutting down a large pine tree gave me a lot of comfort once by parking his pickup truck between the tree and my garage. Our interests were aligned, in that case literally. If the tree fell on my house, it would take out his truck along with it.

Alignment is especially important with external vendors. I once had a team review twenty technology projects with external vendors to discover common factors on the relationships that worked well and on those that hadn't. In summary, we found the following three requirements for the best relationship, and to avoid a bad one:

1. Alignment: Make sure they're incentivized the right way so that you have a shared definition of success. An important detail for vendor alignment is holding back a meaningful portion of payment until the job is completed to your satisfaction.
2. Clear accountability: Have a single point of contact for decision-making and communication both on your side and theirs.
3. Communication: Talk every day. If there's bad news, you want it as early as possible.

Technology development has recently moved to an "Agile" framework that embraces these three concepts, and it works well when executed properly.

 *Align with your vendors and anyone else you're dependent on.* 

Umbrella Coverage

When I headed our mutual fund shop, we had five meetings a year with our board, mostly composed of external board members, to make decisions on keeping or getting rid of portfolio subadvisors or adjusting fees. At every one of these meetings, there was a report from the board's counsel about recent legal developments, and this report often included a summary of recent litigation against fund companies. In one meeting, counsel reviewed two cases with nearly identical fact patterns that provided almost directly contradictory arguments to their lawsuits.

"You invested too conservatively, so I didn't get enough return."

"You invested too aggressively, so you damaged my return."

How do you protect against that? You can't by picking a side or a position, nor through logic. The only defense, and it worked, is to have good, thorough processes, including robust debates, and document them really well. That kept us out of a lot of trouble.

 *Document your processes well and stick to them.* 

Things Are Fine Just as They Are

In chapter 12, I described the risk of complacency, or standing still when others are changing. Here's a simple rule of thumb, which I applied not only to my risk team but also to several lines of business: "If we find ourselves in a meeting where we're laughing at the competition, we'd better think again and look very closely at them. They could be one of our biggest threats."

You've got to shake things up once in a while to avoid complacency.

Stay Out of the Mud

One specific risk that warrants special attention is around branding. It takes years to build a brand but a very short time to destroy it, especially in a world of ever-evolving social media. If you have a reputation for high quality, for instance, you don't want your name connected to a business partner known for low quality. If your brand favors integrity, don't associate with a partner whose reputation is less than scrupulous.

Be aware of the reputation of those you associate with.

You Don't Know What You Don't Know . . .

There are times when you just don't know much about a new venture you're going into, and that presents its own type of risk.

I once took over a new business that was struggling. It was an experiment selling insurance for final needs, the kind you hear about when watching old reruns of *Matlock* or *Murder She Wrote*, with a low premium and limited benefit meant to cover the costs of a funeral and burial. The business had a reputation of being somewhat low-class and dodgy, which was a risk to reputation. However, there was one other issue not related to reputation. In final needs, it's typical to have a cap on how much insurance you can buy because the people who are buying it are usually sick and desperately need it. In an effort to differentiate from competitors, the development team designed a product with a $25,000 cap when the rest of the industry had a $15,000 cap.

Big mistake.

Our mortality rates, even after only a year or two of experience, were running much higher than expected. Luckily, someone had the foresight to limit how much business we wrote and ensure about 90 percent of it was reinsured (shared) with another carrier so that it was on the hook for most of the losses.

 **If you don't know what you're doing, limit your exposure and have someone else in it with you.** 

. . . And I'm Here to Help (Again)

There are certain functions in an organization that aren't always welcome when they show up. Risk teams and audit teams are two examples.

When I first ran a line business and an auditor or risk team came in, my reaction was usually something like this: "Let's get them in

and out of here as quickly as we can so we can get back to real work."
I had good reason for it, having observed a few audit teams who were
rewarded for finding problems and for manufacturing them if there
weren't any.

On the other hand, risk and audit teams often have a cross-organizational perspective that a line manager doesn't, so they can string
things together that a line manager is unaware of. So, if you're part of
one of these teams, you need to build a partnership.

There are limits. You still need to be the stern parent if there's bad
behavior going on, but start with respect, both for the people you're
working with and for the work they do. Ask lots of questions; you
may have a general perspective, but they have the details. Constantly
remind them of what you're trying to accomplish, and make sure it's
the same objective they're trying to reach.

> ***Mutual respect is a key to effective risk
> and audit teams.***

Summary

***Risk is an important component of every decision. Keep
these things in mind when evaluating risk:***

- ***A challenge when assessing risk is that it can be all
  negative. Consider returns and benefits as well.***

- *For a full view of risk, differentiate risk decisions, gather diverse input, and periodically incorporate fresh views.*
- *Take some risks, but pick your shots as to which ones to take.*
- *Avoid open-ended, unrecoverable risk. If you can't afford to lose something, don't put it at risk.*
- *Find ways to assess risks other than incrementally so that they don't sneak up on you.*
- *The real world is populated by people as well as numbers, making human behavior a risk.*
- *Watch for the risk of misalignment, especially of incentives and with third parties.*
- *Documenting your processes can help protect against legal risk.*
- *Stay open to new ideas and threats.*
- *Protect your reputation.*
- *Be aware of your lack of familiarity in an area, and limit or lay off some of the risk when experimenting, especially if stakes are high.*
- *Treat your risk, audit, and compliance teams with respect, and be sure they're aligned.*

Chapter 14

Wanna Trade? (Negotiating)

Some people are drawn to the back-and-forth nature of negotiating as if they're playing a game. As an introvert, I found it intimidating in early career days, especially since my first contract negotiation was on a deal for a third of a billion dollars. That made me seek more information on it, attending three negotiation courses, one with Wharton, one through an advertisement, and one for multiple days at Harvard. Even supplementing those with considerable reading, I felt that I'd only just scratched the surface, until I realized I was building experience.

Of course, every bid and new deal is a negotiation. However, so is almost every meeting or discussion with a colleague or presentation under intense Q&A with the boss. Even outside work, I learned that one view of chess is as a series of continual negotiations made in multiple dimensions. I had more experience than I thought.

In this chapter, we'll review the following questions:

- *Are there specific negotiating tactics I can apply?*
- *What steps can I take to avoid losing too much?*
- *How important are soft skills in negotiating?*

- *Is there an order or plan for negotiating, and if so does it change based on circumstances?*
- *How can I elevate from short-term tactics to longer-term strategic objectives?*

Ready, Aim

In the aforementioned advertised class, maybe twenty-five to thirty people from multiple industries met at a downtown hotel next to the office. The instructor was the kind you'd expect from a class advertised in an in-flight magazine: loud, brash, and hyper-confident. He focused more on negotiation tactics than on strategy or broad principles. That was fine and what I was looking for.

The first exercise split us into pairs, one buyer and one seller, to negotiate the sale of a share of stock. After negotiating for fifteen to twenty minutes, we reviewed the results. Our coach intentionally gave us background information so vague that we couldn't make any kind of proper valuation, either as a buyer or a seller.

The point of that first exercise wasn't to develop negotiating skills but to look at a pattern. When the coach graphed where each side made their opening bid and compared it to results, it was patently obvious: If as a buyer your opening bid was lower, then you purchased at a lower price, and if as a seller your opening bid was high, you sold at a higher price. In other words, there is anchoring that goes on from the outset.

The purported lesson was simple.

 *Ask for more than you expect to get if you're a seller and bid less than where you think you'll end up as a buyer, and you'll get a better result.* 

Fence First, Cattle Later

Another exercise was planning things out before we started, in this case making our best estimates of what an acceptable value would be to either buy or sell, what the bare minimum or maximum bid was, and what our starting bids were. In all three of the negotiating classes, there was this same element of planning.

Regardless of which approach you use, one of the most important factors to consider when you plan is to set your limits in advance. That way you're less likely to give in to the temptation to go beyond your limits in the last 1 percent of negotiation, the ostensible time when 99 percent of negotiators fail to hold their ground.

In chapter 13, I described a near disaster when hiking Mt. Adams, showing that in some cases limits may literally save a life, but they can also be useful in a negotiation.

 *Plan, including setting limits, before you negotiate.* 

Too Rich for My Blood

Along the same lines of preparation, another negotiating lesson was to be aware of how much you might lose.

When I first moved to Maine, the company actuaries were regular gamblers. I never made it to the local horse track with them, but I did frequently join them in some of their poker games. The game was dealer's choice, and as you can imagine with a bunch of mathematicians, some of the games got pretty complicated. I don't ever remember back in the 1980s playing Texas Hold'em, and even Five-Card Draw was rare, but I did see a lot of Chicago Split, Day Baseball, Night Baseball, Lowball, 727, and others. What struck me after a few games was how often our boss, who'd been there a while and had reached a pretty high level in the company, seemed to win. He was a very sharp card player and could read people well, but I think one of the reasons he did so well was that he'd hang in on every contested pot. He had the resources and could afford a loss. If the pot got too rich, I'd have to drop because I hadn't brought enough with me and wanted to buy food the next week. Others had similar limitations.

Your ability to withstand a loss matters.

One of the games we played in Maine was Liar's Poker, with one-dollar bills. The idea is to bluff your opponent, to show strength at all times, to be the one who never gives in. It's a lot like the card game BS (more politely called "Cheat" or "I Doubt It"). In Michael Lewis's 1989 book *Liar's Poker*, he describes the raucous frat boy environment that permeated Wall Street at the time. He recalls when the head of the firm, constantly seeking to intimidate, challenged one of the traders to a single game, mano a mano, for a million dollars. The trader was stuck. If he played and lost, he'd be out more than he could afford, and if he backed down, he'd lose face and look weak. So, he responded the only way he could. He offered to play one game one-on-one, but only for "real money," ten million dollars. The CEO laughed at the "joke" and walked away, and the trader's reputation (dignity is too strong a word) was intact. Playing for $1 million didn't phase the CEO, but playing for $10 million did, and he backed down.

The stakes matter.

Even with great odds, however, not everyone can afford a loss. I once presented at a conference where a couple hundred participants were able to vote with a handheld machine. I offered up a theoretical bet: "We'll flip, and only once, a coin that has been determined to be fair by the American Numismatic Association's coin-flipping standards. If it comes up heads, you pay me one dollar. If it comes up tails, I'll pay you two dollars." How many do you think took that bet? Almost everyone. I then offered the same bet with the same odds but with the stakes raised: "I win ten thousand dollars for heads, and you win twenty thousand dollars for tails." The proportion willing to take the bet dropped dramatically, to around 14 percent, proving that perceived losses can directly influence a negotiation.

 *Be aware of your downside limits going in, and don't put at risk more than what you can afford to lose.* 

Do You Have Something in Your Eye?

We all get nervous when we get to the critical part of a negotiation, and it's common for our nervousness to manifest itself, perhaps in an agitated tic, an eye blink, a rapid pace of talking, or our face getting flushed.

One of our pieces of homework in the first negotiating class was to practice asking for something we might feel is unreasonable so that we could get used to the discomfort that comes with it. I found myself, as instructed, buying a bag of chips at the local convenience store and asking if they'd take a dollar for it instead of $1.19. I even asked for a discount in the cafeteria line at lunch.

An extension of this concept is that negotiation can get emotional. I can still remember the instructor asking, "When your four-year-old yells and screams that they hate you, do they mean it?"

Having a four-year-old at the time, I joined in the chorus of voices answering, "No, of course not."

"Yes!" he corrected us. "Yes, at that moment, in the heat of the moment, they do mean it. Half a minute later, they don't."

 **_Sometimes in negotiations it's best to back out, cool off, and come back to it the next day._** 

Once Again, from the Top

If you ask and are rebuffed, simply ask again.

I had dropped my car at the shop to get a new muffler and practiced my newly acquired negotiating skills. Calmly, and acting as if it were the most reasonable request in the world, I asked for a discount. Apparently recalling his own training, the person behind the counter responded, "No. I'm sorry, but we don't do that here."

We talked a while longer, and I asked again. Surely there must be something they could do. He also must have been trained in what to do if someone asked twice, because almost immediately he said, "Okay. Twenty percent."

 **_Ask twice._** 

The Writing on the Wall

Another lesson that can be useful on either side of a negotiation is that putting something in writing can give you authority.

Take this situation for example: You bought an outfit, and before trying it on you discover that someone gave you the same one as a gift. You go to return the duplicate, and the store clerk points to the policy written on the wall behind them that reads, "Store credit only."

"Ignore it," said our sage. "Just keep asking. They'll usually give in."

My wife worked for eleven different retail brands. It's true.

On the other side of the equation is this: If someone asks you for money, a donation you're not interested in giving, or something similarly uncomfortable, change your response from "No" to "I'm sorry, but I have a policy to donate only to charities that I've selected at the beginning of the year," or whatever similar reference you require. As soon as you have a policy, it's like a written sign. You don't have to explain the policy. It has authority just by existing.

 *Policies, especially in writing, imply authority.* 

Talk This Way

One more lesson is, be nice.

Suppose you're shopping for furniture and would like a discount. One approach is saying, "This piece is damaged. It has a scratch across it. I'd like a discount" or "I'm not sure it's that well made. Can you knock off ten percent?" The proprietor, especially in a small local shop, is likely to feel at best backed into a corner and at worst insulted by the implication that they don't know quality.

An alternative with better prospects is to say, "I really like this piece, but it's a bit more than what I'd planned to spend. Can you *help me out* a little?" People love to help. I used this phrase the very morning I wrote this paragraph, and I received a discount. I also once picked up a $1,200 dining room table for $400 using this approach.

Sometimes it doesn't work, but what's the harm in asking as long as you do it with respect?

> ***Ask for help, and do so nicely.***

The Power to Choose

Another suggestion is to present options. You see people do this with their kids all the time, such as when they say things like, "Do you want to walk holding my hand or sit in the cart?"

I had a chance to use this tactic with a failing block of business that had been around for a long time and was always losing money. We'd tried to reprice it several times, but the company had 8,500 affiliated agents who wielded tremendous influence. Many were millionaires, and the pressure they put on executives was akin to that of a strong union. In the spirit of both presenting options and starting closer to where we wanted to end up, we offered to either shut down the business or significantly reprice it to get it back to being profitable.

They took the repricing option, as long they could have better pricing than independent (unaffiliated) agents.

> ***Provide options.***

Going Green

Counterintuitively, lack of knowledge can sometimes be a benefit. In their book *Made to Stick*, Chip and Dan Heath describe the "curse of knowledge," meaning we limit our thinking because we already presume the answer. In negotiations, the opposite can be not only true but helpful. If you don't know enough to be wary of something, what might be distasteful or even reckless in someone more experienced can be a good fit for the naive.

An example was that first huge contract negotiation I had with two professional negotiators at one of the nation's largest companies. At the time, it seemed foolish to put somebody as green as I was on such a large contract. I later learned that my naivete was the very reason I was assigned the task. A new negotiator (with circumscribed authority) will fight tooth and nail for every provision, not wanting to give in on anything that might risk both their reputation and career, nor the company's welfare. An experienced negotiator will often jump to an answer because they're familiar with the territory and know where things are going to end up. In other words, they concede too much.

I did fight for every provision, often well into the night and with Dan and Daniel, neither of whom I ever met in person nor whose faces I saw, and we closed the deal with a solid contract.

 *Consider putting a new person on a negotiation but with limited authority.* 

What's It Worth to You?

One of my friends who was also a coworker came into the office beaming one day. When I asked why, he told me he'd managed to dispose of some old tires. What excited him wasn't that he'd gotten rid of them. It was how he'd done it.

Not wanting to visit the dump, he left the tires at the curb with a sign that read, "Free." They sat there for two weeks. Just the prior evening, he'd changed the sign to read, "Four tires. Used. $25 each." When he pulled out of the driveway that morning for work, they were gone! They'd been stolen during the night.

Another friend had his house on the market for eighteen months and couldn't sell it. When he raised the price by about $30,000, he got an offer the next day.

> **Be aware of the actions you take that indicate value.**

You're Up

When it comes to tactics, there's the age-old question of whether you should make the first offer or let someone else do it. There are certainly situations in which starting first and anchoring expectations can help, but the generally accepted tenet of not going first often pays off.

Just before Hurricane Katrina hit, my wife and I decided to replace our dying Isuzu Rodeo. We wanted to buy used to save money, and we settled on a Toyota Sequoia. I looked at multiple cars online and finally found one at a local dealer. I thoroughly researched what

I considered a good price, a great price, my starting bid, and my highest offer before going into the dealer. I even went in near the end of the month so the dealer would be interested in selling the car to hit sales goals. Finally, my wife and I agreed in advance that whatever offer we got, she would shake her head and say that she was really more interested in the (imaginary) other car we'd seen instead of the Sequoia.

The salesperson showed us two or three vehicles, including the one we were interested in, and asked me to make an offer. Remembering not to go first and that he was a professional negotiator, I attempted to demur.

"Anything," he said. "Just give me a number to start with."

"I'm sorry. I did some research, but I can't remember what I saw was a reasonable price. Why don't you let me know what you're expecting for it."

He went into the dreaded backroom for a few minutes, then came out and offered me a price lower than the number I'd pegged as the best possible deal I might get if everything went perfectly. I shook my head in disappointment, my wife played her part, and we negotiated downward from there. We got a fantastic deal, and we ended up putting about 350,000 miles on that car before we let it go.

In another situation, this time at work, one of our salesmen had recently completed an arrangement for a real estate account with what started as an internal negotiation. He had talked the actuaries into a certain price, let's call it fifty basis points (0.50 percent per year), insisting he needed a number that low to get the sale. He walked into the meeting with all the contracts drafted up at fifty, pointed to his briefcase, and indicated that he had signature-ready documents inside.

Looking concerned, his prospective client shook his head, then surprised him with, "If you didn't get down to seventy, I'm not signing anything."

Genuinely taken aback, and knowing he had documents that were much better than the desired seventy, he paused, opened the briefcase, took out the contract (at fifty), and ripped it up, saying, "I'm too embarrassed to show you what I've got here. I'll go back and push to get you down to seventy."

> ***It's usually a good idea to let the other person speak first.***

Listen Up

In the Wharton negotiation training, we engaged in an exercise similar to that in the airline ad's class: a mock negotiation. Upon completion, the noted correlation was a different one, though. In this case, the best deals were struck by the negotiations that took the longest time, by those who persisted and never gave up, those who, critically, kept asking questions and letting the other side talk. You can't find out what's most important to the person you're negotiating with unless you find out their motivation.

One example may have been apocryphal. A man had purchased a high-end vehicle, a Porsche I believe, for something like $3,000. He wondered whether it had been stolen, but when he asked the seller, he found out she had just completed a vicious divorce and was selling the car cheap as a way to get back at her ex. The man bought it and got a great deal.

In his book *Never Split the Difference*, Chris Voss, a former top FBI negotiator, characterizes listening as the main prerequisite to successful negotiation. He recommends that after having duly prepared in advance and during the early stages of actual discussions, you should forget entirely what you're planning to say to get your own position across and instead focus solely on listening to the other person.

 *Listen to find out what's most important to the person you're negotiating with.* 

A Principles-Based Approach

Harvard's executive education negotiation program, populated by high-ranking execs from all over the country, was led by world-famous negotiator and author William Ury, who initiated the well-known win–win approach. Ury has spent time with and/or advised the Dalai Lama, President Carter, and the Colombian government and has been on both sides in multiple conflicts. His approach was more principles-based and less tactical. For example, he described some of the previous methods I've mentioned as haggling, not negotiation. Haggling is negotiating in one dimension, such as simply debating price. It's also focused on the short-term, and there's a winner and a loser. A negotiation with a short-term focus on establishing a winner and a loser may leave the "losing" side with a feeling of resentment that dictates against a long-term relationship. One of the reasons for World War II was the Germans resenting the Treaty of Versailles at the end of World War I.

If you're in a one-time transaction with a stranger, haggling is okay. But if you expect continued interaction, you should negotiate instead, in multiple dimensions and in good faith, based on what's important to both parties. In mathematics, there's a concept of finding maxima and minima at extremes. In negotiation, the best outcome for both sides happens when each side gets more of what they want instead of compromising where each gives something up. Think of loss aversion or Solomon's famous judgment that no one wins with half a baby.

Ury started with a simple exercise to teach us how to say no. One side asked for something, and the other side had to refuse. The challenge? Even after three minutes, half the groups couldn't make it through without giving in.

Over the next few days, Ury expanded on this with a strategy I remember with my own mnemonic, NBA (like basketball):

- N = No. Simply say, "I don't accept your offer."
- B = Because. Give a reason for saying no. For example, "I can't complete that project by next week because I have other priorities."
- A = Alternative. Offer another solution, such as, "I could do it in a week if you talk to the CEO."

This approach works well for any situation, even small ones like being asked to speak at a conference.

Ury also recommends planning ahead, including making a list of strengths for both sides and thinking about what each one fears or wants to avoid. In addition, he suggests developing good back-up alternatives if you can't reach a negotiated agreement. For example, a company looking to buy a large plant had a backup plan to buy smaller plants instead. They ended up going with the smaller plants because they liked that option more, even though it wasn't their first choice.

Similar to Katy Milkman's advice of imagining what you'd tell someone else in the same situation, Ury emphasized removing emotion from negotiations because this psychological distance helps you make more objective decisions. He also pointed out that there are many layers to negotiations, and not all of them are readily apparent. He shared a story of an NYC hostage negotiator who never lost a hostage. In one case, the gunman walked out yelling at officers, but once he was in the cruiser he thanked the negotiator for letting him maintain face in front of his gang.

Ury closed the class with a comment that resonated: "Almost every conflict, whether large or small, stems from a perceived lack of respect."

A key to successful conflict resolution, then, is to respect the person or organization you're negotiating with. I'm sure you've heard that one before.

 **Negotiate in multiple dimensions for a positive long-term relationship.** 

Summary

Negotiations are much more complex and multidimensional than many people realize. Whether bargaining in a one-time transaction or negotiating in what will likely become a long-term relationship, look to apply some of these specific techniques:

- *Start high, end high. Start low, end low.*
- *Set strategy and limits in advance.*
- *Don't risk more than you can afford to lose.*
- *Don't let your emotions cloud your negotiating judgment. Back off if you need to.*
- *When rebuffed, ask again.*
- *As a consumer, consider whether implied authority is genuine. When offering or responding to others, use implied authority if you need to.*
- *Be nice. Show respect for the person you're negotiating (or bargaining) with.*
- *Offer options.*
- *Be aware of how you indicate value.*
- *Usually, wait for the first offer, unless you need to anchor the bidding.*
- *Listen and ask to find out what's most important to your negotiating partner.*
- *Beware the short-term "win" with long-term adverse implications.*
- *Remember NBA: No, Because, Alternative.*
- *Think about alternatives if you can't reach agreement, even if it's daunting to do so.*
- *Negotiate for the long-term, and consider all dimensions that are available to trade.*

Conclusion:
A Roadmap to a
Successful Career

We started this book with a sense of how we best learn and what keeps us interested in learning. One invaluable technique is to take a breath once in a while, step back, and see whether you identify any patterns. After writing this treatise and looking back on it, I see a few threads to the tapestry that appear again and again.

First is that you are not alone. Even if you're hyper-focused on yourself and your own development, your progress and success are dependent on your relationship with others. If you get smarter or better at your job but the business fails, it's neither internally nor externally rewarding. Similarly, if you treat your career as if you're alone on an island, you won't get anything near as much accomplished nor learn or improve as much as when you interact with those around you.

Within that framework, certain fundamental principles apply. You want to maintain integrity, both so that you make better decisions and so that people will know what you stand for and listen to you:

- Gathering information from multiple sources is better than a single detailed view.

- You've got to get your hands dirty and see things up close.
- True partnership means when you win, everyone around you wins.

Finally, there are specific techniques you can use that have a higher likelihood of success than others, whether with decision-making, motivating people, developing relationships, improving processes, making career decisions, growing or fixing a business, coming up with new ideas, building a team, or helping others.

Might you discover some other approach that's even better? I hope so! Please do, and please share it as widely as possible when you find it.

Many good history books provide a map for readers to refer to for reinforcement. I've included one on the next page that summarizes everything we've been through, and I sincerely hope you use it often.

Here's an alternative way to summarize everything we've been through:

- **To Teach Is to Learn**

  Though the saying "To teach is to learn" was first described to me as Japanese in origin, it's also ascribed to Seneca the Younger from two thousand years ago, as well as to a French moralist named Joubert. I suspect all may be true. Regardless of its derivation, I think of it simply as this: You don't really understand something completely until you can explain it to someone else so that they "get it." Take teaching my kids how to ride a bike, for example. I didn't recall how many steps there were until trying to help them understand and succeed. They had to learn how to stand over the bike to get on, how the kickstand works, how to point the wheel, and where the pedals are positioned all

Roadmap to a Successful Career

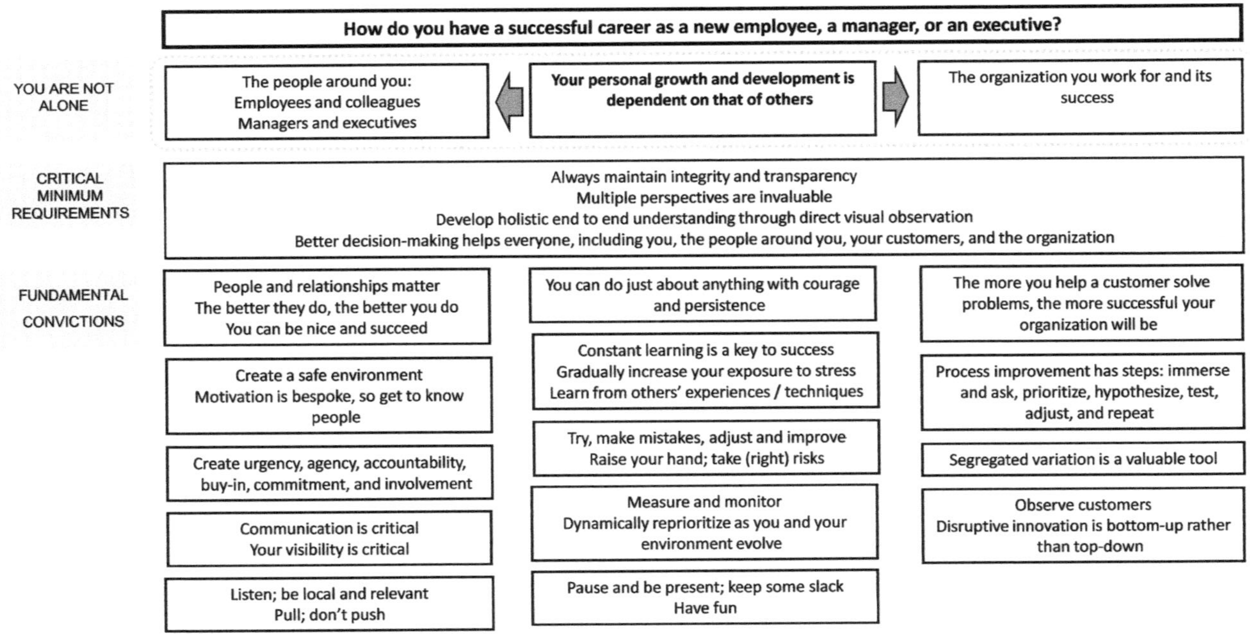

How do you have a successful career as a new employee, a manager, or an executive?

YOU ARE NOT ALONE

The people around you:
Employees and colleagues
Managers and executives

Your personal growth and development is dependent on that of others

The organization you work for and its success

CRITICAL MINIMUM REQUIREMENTS

Always maintain integrity and transparency
Multiple perspectives are invaluable
Develop holistic end to end understanding through direct visual observation
Better decision-making helps everyone, including you, the people around you, your customers, and the organization

FUNDAMENTAL CONVICTIONS

People and relationships matter
The better they do, the better you do
You can be nice and succeed

You can do just about anything with courage and persistence

The more you help a customer solve problems, the more successful your organization will be

Create a safe environment
Motivation is bespoke, so get to know people

Constant learning is a key to success
Gradually increase your exposure to stress
Learn from others' experiences / techniques

Process improvement has steps: immerse and ask, prioritize, hypothesize, test, adjust, and repeat

Create urgency, agency, accountability, buy-in, commitment, and involvement

Try, make mistakes, adjust and improve
Raise your hand; take (right) risks

Segregated variation is a valuable tool

Communication is critical
Your visibility is critical

Measure and monitor
Dynamically reprioritize as you and your environment evolve

Observe customers
Disruptive innovation is bottom-up rather than top-down

Listen; be local and relevant
Pull; don't push

Pause and be present; keep some slack
Have fun

before they got anywhere near balancing without falling over. That doesn't mean that the best way to teach is to explain every step; you'll lose somebody right out of the gate. But I didn't really know what it took to ride a bike until trying to explain it.

- **To Give Is to Receive**

A true gift is one you give without expecting anything in return, and that act of giving sometimes delivers as much, and sometimes more, joy to you as to the recipient. Your face lights up because you see someone you love being excited. My uncle had a corollary: If someone gives you something and it's a true and genuine gift, accept it. Let them pay for that meal. You know by accepting that you're bringing them joy. There's even psychological evidence backing this up. One of the best ways to get a sense of progress and control in tough times is to volunteer to help others.

- **To Love Is to Live**

Even if you succeed wildly, achieving everything you've aimed for, it's superficial until you share it with someone. Parents and grandparents share their experiences with the generations that come after. Teachers share knowledge. Partners are excited by each other's success. You don't have success, or a life, until it's shared.

Good luck to you as you apply these principles, and happy learning!

Acknowledgments

I'd like to thank the following folks for making it possible to publish this book.

Upon my retirement, Danielle Steele Bolt and Colleen Dennis presented me with the gift of Storyworth, which encouraged me to capture many more stories than are in this book, both personal and work-related. It has been therapeutic to relive them and to share them with family and colleagues. Those stories formed the backbone of this book.

Jamala Arland, Mido Osman, and Geoff Keast provided many insightful comments on a bloated and cumbersome first draft and helped reorient the text to be more useful to readers.

A mini focus group of friends and family helped supplement those I've already mentioned to concentrate content and presentation on the areas most meaningful to aspiring leaders, in a way that is accessible and attractive. Thank you to Jenny Ball, Jay Butler, Sue Butler, Matt Grisevich, Mike Grisevich, Sean Haendiges, Tonesha Haendiges, Caitlin Krzykowski, Paul Krzykowski, Brian Lochner, Jeff Lochner, and Amy Tran.

Everyone who contributed a testimonial did so as a result of direct or indirect involvement with one of the stories in this book. Thank you to Tom McInerney, Ron Edwards, Amy Tran,

Mido Osman, Pete Vatev, Jeff Lochner, Amanda Hug, Elaine Sarsynski, Matt Grisevich, Barb March, Darrin Tulley, Diane Lopes, Adam Hallet and Tracy Ann Shaw.

Jenn Grace and her entire team at Publish Your Purpose, including a dogged and organized Alexander Loutsenko, kept me on track, and Jenn's book on writing lifted my spirits and kept me going when I got down.

My developmental editor, Anna Heim, patiently worked with me to streamline the content, even when I bristled at someone else's helpful commentary. My copy editor, Nancy Graham-Tillman, a living compendium of style and grammar, polished subsequent drafts. The end result is vastly better than what I started with thanks to both of them.

Cover designer Marke, proofreader Lily and typesetter Sundar paid special attention to detail which is important, but which I had no idea existed.

I'm grateful to all those really good teachers, bosses, and mentors who encouraged continual learning and motivation, among them Joe, Marion, Reinhard, Don, Anne, Gordon, Chris, Brian, Elaine, and Tom who stand out.

Literally hundreds of colleagues and employees have created the stories herein. It was a pleasure to work with you, and I learned from you too.

My family and friends have been terrific with their continuing support and encouragement. You kept me going.

Last is a special thank you to my wife of nearly thirty-eight years, Annmarie, who passed away in 2021. Your love and support got me back to work for the capstone of a long career, and your fierce determination and good humor in difficult circumstances were a model for how to be all-in and get the most out of the life we have. Thank you, Am.

Recommended Reading and Listening

Behavioral Finance/Behavioral Economics

- *How to Change: The Science of Getting from Where You Are to Where You Want to Be* by Katy Milkman is an engaging summary of how to make better decisions. She also has an excellent podcast called *Choiceology*.
- *Misbehaving: The Making of Behavioral Economics* by Richard H. Thaler is a summary of his life's work that won him a Nobel Prize.
- *Nudge: Improving Decisions About Health, Wealth, and Happiness* by Richard H. Thaler and Cass R. Sunstein is an overview of design architecture and how "benign paternalism" can help people make better decisions.
- *Predictably Irrational: The Hidden Forces That Shape Our Decisions* by Dan Ariely is an easy read on some of the seemingly crazy decisions we make. The television show *Irrational* is based on his work.
- *Thinking, Fast and Slow* by Daniel Kahneman is a tour de force overview of the life's work of one of the founders of modern decision theory. Almost every chapter left me awestruck and second-guessing how I make my own decisions.

Decision-Making

- *The Paradox of Choice: Why More Is Less* by Barry Schwartz explains why more choice often results in fewer and poorer decisions and offers ideas for what to do about it.

Design

- *A Whole New Mind: Why Right-Brainers Will Rule the Future* by Daniel H. Pink is a discussion of the emerging need to blend creative problem-solving with analytical skills. It's excellent especially if you have a kid with a creative streak (and they all have one). Also, his book *Drive* is great for motivation.
- *The Design of Everyday Things* by Don Norman is a discussion of design principles and contains many examples of both good and poor design with the customer at the center.
- *Why We Buy: The Science of Shopping* by Paco Underhill is an overview of techniques that improve buying behavior, again with a focus on the customer.

Identifying Patterns and Trends

- *Antifragile: Things That Gain from Disorder* by Nicholas Taleb is a moderately heavy-handed but unique treatise positing that we should expect chaotic events (coined "black swans") and prepare for them.
- *Extraordinary Popular Delusions and the Madness of Crowds* by Charles Mackay gives an overview of trends, fads, and bubbles over the several hundred years prior to its publication in 1841. History repeated itself, even back then.
- *How to Lie with Statistics* by Darrell Huff has an explanation of tricks marketers and propagandists use that holds up well seventy years later.

- *Liar's Poker: Rising through the Wreckage on Wall Street* by Michael Lewis gives a history of the go-go days of the bond market in the 1980s, with fascinating cultural insights about getting pulled into something and having a hard time letting go.
- Malcolm Gladwell's three books *The Tipping Point, Blink,* and *Outliers* are ones I've enjoyed and found insight in, just as in all his books. I also enjoy listening to Gladwell speak. He provides a new way of looking at traditional data and approaches.

Innovation

- *Blue Ocean Strategy: How to Create Uncontested Market Space and Make the Competition Irrelevant* by W. Chan Kim and Renée Mauborgne provides advice on how to stop focusing on the most expensive aspects of competition and give the customer more of what they really want.
- *David and Goliath: Underdogs, Misfits, and the Art of Battling Giants* by Malcolm Gladwell provides the explanation that very often the only way around a problem, especially if the odds are stacked against you, is something unconventional.
- *The Creative Thinker's Toolkit* by Gerard Puccio offers some practical resources for generating ideas and then narrowing them down.
- *The Innovator's Dilemma: When New Technologies Cause Great Firms to Fail* by Clayton M. Christensen, and *The Innovator's Solution: Creating and Sustaining Successful Growth* by Clayton M. Christensen and Michael E. Raynor offer clear explanations of how disruptive innovation occurs, how to spot it, and the challenges and suggested approaches for implementing it yourself.

- *Why Not?: How to Use Everyday Ingenuity to Solve Problems Big and Small* by Barry Nalebuff and Ian Ayres provides techniques for generating creative ideas and gives many examples.

Motivation and Influence

- *Bringing Out the Best in People: How to Apply the Astonishing Power of Positive Reinforcement* by Aubrey C. Daniels gives specific dos and don'ts when it comes to motivation.

- *Green Eggs and Ham* by Dr. Seuss is a go-to manual of persistence coupled with a positive attitude.

- *How to Talk So Kids Will Listen & Listen So Kids Will Talk* by Adele Faber and Elaine Mazlish offers great practical, implementable advice on motivating people, teams, and especially kids.

- *Influence: The Psychology of Persuasion* by Robert Cialdini is an easy read that summarizes some innate human behaviors, how they're used for good or ill, and how to protect against misuse.

- *Made to Stick: Why Some Ideas Survive and Others Die* by Chip Heath and Dan Heath provides a half dozen extremely useful tools to help get your point across and have it remembered. It's entertaining and fun as well as valuable.

Negotiating

- *Getting to Yes: Negotiating Agreement Without Giving In* by Roger Fisher, William L. Ury, and Bruce Patton offers an approach to negotiation focused on mutual understanding and advantage.

- *Never Split the Difference: Negotiating as If Your Life Depended on It* by Chris Voss and Tahl Raz contains techniques from an FBI negotiator focused on listening, tactical empathy, and getting beyond "yes" to "and how."

About the Author

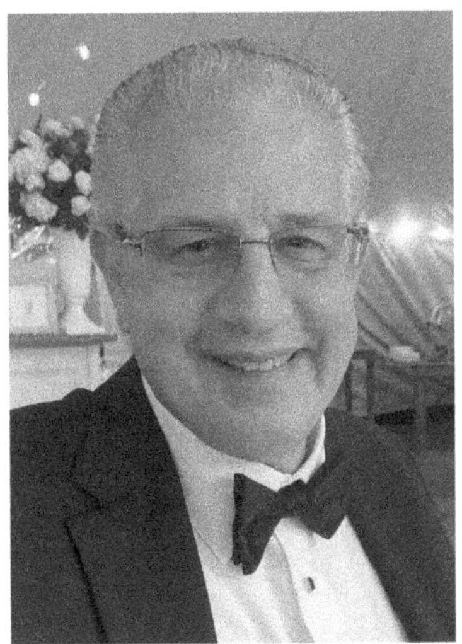

Brian's 40+ year career with half a dozen Fortune 500 financial services and insurance companies provided the opportunity to learn the hard way from a host of good leaders, mentors, peers, employees, and customers, and in a wide variety of roles: innovation and new product development, marketing, sales, product management, operational infrastructure, investments, start-ups, growth, turnarounds, wind-downs, risk management, and executive leadership.

He has reaped the benefits of learning in multiple media: at the kitchen table, in academic settings, on the job, facing someone trying to kick or punch him, over the chessboard, taking apart a bicycle to repair the brakes, struggling to understand a doctor's instructions in Spanish for a toddler, almost collapsing atop two mountains (and actually doing so on a Costa Rican adventure), reading copiously, experimenting, asking questions, talking with friends, strangers, family and home repair specialists, remaining insatiably curious, and caring for a terminally ill spouse.

After some significant life changes, he's now seeking to fill every day with something meaningful for himself and others, including fulfilling a promise to share some of his many often-requested stories and lessons with you.

In addition to writing fiction and non-fiction, Brian enjoys teaching and learning in classes on Cape Cod, brushing up foreign language skills at home and abroad, trying to put notes together on a piano keyboard again after a 50-year break, advising and celebrating success with friends and former colleagues, traveling, and spending time with his family.

The B Corp Movement

Dear reader,

Thank you for reading this book and joining the Publish Your Purpose community! You are joining a special group of people who aim to make the world a better place.

What's Publish Your Purpose About?

Our mission is to elevate the voices often excluded from traditional publishing. We intentionally seek out authors and storytellers with diverse backgrounds, life experiences, and unique perspectives to publish books that will make an impact in the world.

Beyond our books, we are focused on tangible, action-based change. As a woman- and LGBTQ+-owned company, we are committed to reducing inequality, lowering levels of poverty, creating a healthier environment, building stronger communities, and creating high-quality jobs with dignity and purpose.

As a Certified B Corporation, we use business as a force for good. We join a community of mission-driven companies building a more equitable, inclusive, and sustainable global economy. B Corporations must meet high standards of transparency, social and environmental performance, and accountability as determined by the nonprofit B Lab. The certification process is rigorous and ongoing (with a recertification requirement every three years).

How Do We Do This?

We intentionally partner with socially and economically disadvantaged businesses that meet our sustainability goals. We embrace and encourage our authors and employee's differences in race, age, color, disability, ethnicity, family or marital status, gender identity or expression, language, national origin, physical and mental ability, political affiliation, religion, sexual orientation, socio-economic status, veteran status, and other characteristics that make them unique.

Community is at the heart of everything we do—from our writing and publishing programs to contributing to social enterprise nonprofits like reSET (https://www.resetco.org/) and our work in founding B Local Connecticut.

We are endlessly grateful to our authors, readers, and local community for being the driving force behind the equitable and sustainable world we are building together.

To connect with us online, or publish with us,
visit us at www.publishyourpurpose.com.

Elevating Your Voice,

Jenn T. Grace
Founder, Publish Your Purpose